The Sober Alcoholic

THE SOBER ALCOHOLIC

An Organizational Analysis
of Alcoholics Anonymous

IRVING PETER GELLMAN

———

COLLEGE AND UNIVERSITY PRESS
NEW HAVEN, CONNECTICUT

To

K.

R.

AND

F.

Preface

In the relatively brief span of time since its inception in 1935, Alcoholics Anonymous has achieved international renown. It is not surprising to note the proliferation of literature, both lay and professional, devoted to the accomplishments of the organization. In addition to being acclaimed as a potent force in the rehabilitation of problem drinkers, Alcoholics Anonymous has had a profound influence on the theoretical and methodological issues in the field of alcoholism.

Most of the reports dealing with the association are of a laudatory nature and generally focus on the therapeutic aspects of the fellowship. The relatively few empirical studies to date have been limited in scope, usually examining one or two specific variables within the overall system. A comprehensive, scholarly analysis of the total organizational complex has never been undertaken. This study, based upon two years of field research, is the first such endeavor.

This enterprise would not have been realized without the considerable encouragement of a great many people to whom the author is indebted. Among them Frederick W. Henssler, colleague and friend, has been a constant source of inspiration. Lewis J. Siegal has provided many invaluable insights, particularly within his field of psychiatry. Above all, an abiding debt of gratitude is owed Erwin O. Smigel for giving so generously of his time and counsel throughout this project. Thanks are extended to Dorothy Morris Wahl for her extraordinary talent in typing this manuscript for what must have seemed like an endless number of times.

The author shall always be grateful to the members of the East End group of Alcoholics Anonymous for "sharing their experience, strength, and hope." In order to respect the A.A. tradition of anonymity pseudonyms have been used for the group and its members.

I.P.G.

Contents

Introduction

In 1935, two alcoholics met in Akron, Ohio. They were able to offer each other support in combating their common affliction. Out of this experience the fellowship of Alcoholics Anonymous was founded. At the present time there are about 10,000 A.A. groups throughout the world. There are 7,500 A.A. groups in the United States with 400 local units in the New York metropolitan area.

In 1960, to commemorate the first quarter-century of A.A.'s existence, the Advertising Council set aside the period of June 27th through July 3rd as A.A. Week. Some three thousand radio stations, six hundred television stations, and thousands of newspapers spread the message of this remarkable organization.[1]

Even earlier, coincident with the fifteenth anniversary of A.A., the editors of *Fortune* cited the outstanding growth of the association.

The American tradition of adverse beginnings was fulfilled by this organization which today equally fulfills the tradition of success after struggle. By birthplace, heritage, traditions, habits, looks and tone of voice Alcoholics Anonymous is unmistakably American. And yet in almost every way it contradicts the stencils by which non-American minds gauge American achievement.

It has almost no money and wishes it could do with still less. In fifteen years its membership has grown from nothing to 120,000 yet it never urges anyone to join. Of formal organization it has almost none and it avers that it ought never to have any. A man or woman becomes a member by simple declaration. There are no pledges or constraints in A.A., no records that must be kept or quotas that must be broken. Seniority confers no favors. A.A. has only one purpose—to help the sick alcoholic recover if he wishes. . . . Its members, who know better than to contradict the psychiatrists' diagnosis that they are grandiose, infantile and self-absorbed, practice daily an obedience that has no enforcement mechanism and no system of punishment for infractions.[2]

The *Fortune* statement is journalistic and tends to exaggerate some of the characteristics of A.A. Nevertheless, the preceding acknowledgments indicate the extent of the public recognition of the accomplishments of Alcoholics Anonymous as a rehabilitative agency for problem drinkers.

A.A. may be categorized primarily as a distinct type of voluntary association. Fox classifies such associations as majoral, minoral, and medial organizations.

> Majoral associations are those which serve the interests of the major institutions of society. Business, professional, scientific, educational, labor and agricultural associations are all in this category. Minoral associations on the other hand, are those which serve the interests of significant minorities of the population: women's clubs, fraternal groups, hobby clubs and associations formed to protect the rights of various ethnic minorities in the population are all examples. Finally, medial organizations mediate between various segments of the population. Social welfare groups which mediate between the community and the underprivileged population, veteran's groups, which mediate between veterans and the government, and voluntary health associations, which mediate both between research scientists and the public and between individuals suffering from a disease or disorder and the medical profession, are examples of medial associations.[3]

Alcoholics Anonymous does not specifically fit any one of the ideal types described above but, nevertheless, its singular organizational characteristics properly categorize it as a voluntary association.

Sills classifies national voluntary organizations from the structural point of view "as consisting of two broad types: those which have local units and those whose membership is comprised of individuals living in different parts of the country. National organizations which have local units may in turn be divided into two categories: those which consist of a national headquarters and local branches and those which are federations of semi-autonomous local affiliates."[4] Alcoholics Anonymous belongs to the latter category.

In contemporary times one response to certain forms of deviant behavior—generally those considered by society as the most serious—has been the evolution of specialized control agencies which Goffman calls the "total institution."[5] He notes that "their encompassing or total character is symbolized by the barrier to social intercourse with the outside that is often built right into the physical plant."[6]

Among the "total institutions" in our society are those which have been established for the purpose of confining such diverse elements of the deviant population as the mentally ill and the criminals. Such institutions are marked by a number of significant characteristics.

> First, all aspects of life are conducted in the same place and under the same single authority. Second, each phase of the member's daily activity will be carried out in the immediate company of a large batch of others, all of whom are treated alike and required to do the same thing together. Third, all phases of the day's activities are tightly scheduled with one activity leading at a prearranged time into the next, the whole circle of activities being imposed from above through a system of explicit formal rulings and a body of officials. Finally, the contents of the various enforced activities are brought together as parts of a single overall rational plan purportedly designed to fulfill the official aims of the institution.[7]

Many alcoholics whose drinking had become serious enough to interfere with the performance of their regular social roles often found themselves in such a setting. Frequently their alcoholism led them to a prison or a mental hospital.

However, Alcoholics Anonymous embodies a contrasting theoretical approach to such forms of social control and rehabilitation. First, the members are volunteers who affiliate with the organization of their own free will. Second, the members are not confined or isolated from the general society. Third, the members are not under the supervision of a special staff. Functions of the staff are performed by the members themselves who have also acquired rehabilitative expertise. Fourth, the actors are highly involved and generally participate in the activities of the organization. Finally, the members retain their individuality and personal identity—and assume the role of the sober alcoholic.

These features describe some of the unique aspects of the A.A. system. We are concerned with such factors as they contribute to the formulation of a sociological theory of organization. Within this frame of reference attention focuses on what Bakke calls the "bonds of organization" which comprise the following components:

1. Job specifications and requirements.
2. The communication system.
3. The system of rewards and punishments.
4. The status system.
5. The organizational charter. This refers to the image which appears in the minds of a group as they reflect on the purposes, achievements, traditions and symbols of the group.[8]

In this context Parsons proposes three major themes: the organizational structure; the mobilization of resources; and the mechanisms of implementation.[9] Our analysis of the A.A. organization includes consideration of these elements.

A comprehensive analysis has never been systematically utilized in any previous study of A.A. nor, for that matter, has there ever been an abundance of research devoted to the organization. Despite the extraordinary and highly favorable publicity which Alcoholics Anonymous has received in recent years, most reports dealing with the association have been highly journalistic. There is considerable material to be found in novels, movies, and television with reference to A.A.'s contribution to the problem of alcoholism. The limited number of scientific documents has almost exclusively been devoted to the therapeutic forces in A.A.[10]

A review of the professional literature supports this view and reveals the paucity of available data. Hugh S. Thompson, a non-alcoholic, organized an A.A. group and reports considerable success in assisting in its growth and development.[11] Bales, in an early report, discusses some of the salient characteristics of A.A. which make it an effective rehabilitative force.[12] His commentary is primarily a description of the therapeutic elements of the organization. The same can be said of an article by Bacon which is descriptive of some of the factors operative in A.A.[13] Trice also contributes a report on the features of the A.A. system.[14] In addition, two unpublished doctoral dissertations largely focus on the treatment and recovery aspects of the A.A. system but add few significant insights.[15]

In a more critical vein, Alan Buttin expresses considerable skepticism concerning the effectiveness of A.A. His is one of the rare articles which questions the validity of some of the claims made by Alcoholics Anonymous.[16] Shipley, Jackson, and Boyes report on the therapeutic factors in A.A. from the psychiatric point of view, summing up the comparisons usually made between A.A. and orthodox psychiatry.[17] The authors believe that A.A. embodies many psychiatric principles, particularly those of group therapy. This position is supported in an article by Trice in which he evaluates group therapeutic factors which are part of the A.A. system.[18]

From a more sociological point of view Trice has contributed two statements dealing with the processes which inhibit or encourage affiliation with Alcoholics Anonymous.[19] He attempts to determine what kind of people find it easier to join A.A. and what personality characteristics apparently interfere with such participation. The evidence is not conclusive in any respect. A recent study by Lofland and Lejeune examines the emerging social stratification system in Alcoholics Anonymous.[20] Their findings indicate that there are definite social class distinctions among different A.A. groups.

The paucity of authenticated data, as indicated above, can be attributed directly to the unique character of the structure of Alcoholics Anonymous. Most organizational studies depend largely upon a variety of sources of "inside" information. Social scientists have often been employed by institutions which they have subsequently studied. In other cases interviews, records, and reports have been made freely available to researchers. The publication of the results of such investigations has usually been encouraged. However, A.A. has not been so readily accessible for objective research nor has it invited more rigorous organizational analysis. Alcoholics Anonymous is not a professional or scientific discipline and is under no obligation to subject itself to more precise standards of evaluation. Although it has co-operated with agencies interested in the treatment of the alcoholic and has contributed speakers to forums and meetings on alcoholism, these practices do not enhance scientific organizational analysis.

The chief factor inhibiting research in this area is the stigma still attached to being labeled an alcoholic. Such social deviants understandably resist public and scientific scrutiny.

THE METHOD AND SCOPE OF THE STUDY

The aims of this study required a detailed social anthropological analysis of Alcoholics Anonymous. The classic research technique used for this purpose is, of course, participant observation which the writer utilized. The author could also make use of his previous knowledge of A.A. which he gained when, as personnel director of a sales organization, he accompanied an executive of the firm, who had a drinking problem, to a number of A.A. meetings.

At the outset visits to various A.A. groups were undertaken. These groups appeared to be basically identical in performance characteristics. It was decided that the research would focus on an intensive analysis of one A.A. unit supplemented by observations of other A.A. groups and facilities. Discussions with A.A. members and participation in A.A. functions provided additional data concerning the total system.

In September, 1958, the writer commenced his field work at the East End group of A.A. The group met twice weekly and for the first two months the writer primarily familiarized himself with the personnel and organizational procedures. The officers and members were aware that the author was a college professor preparing a manuscript about A.A. For the duration of the project, field notes were recorded after each session.

The field work covered the following activities over a two-year period:

1. Attendance at a total of 205 meetings of the East End and other A.A. groups.
2. Eight visits to the A.A. ward at Town's Hospital, New York City.
3. Fourteen "twelfth step"[21] calls in conjunction with members of the East End group.
4. Six visits to A.A. meetings at mental institutions.
5. Social interaction with A.A. members, many of whom have become personal friends.
6. Participation in founding a new local group.

Because this is the first comprehensive analysis of Alcoholics Anonymous, much of the report is concerned with detailed observations and data. In a pioneer study of this sort one is obliged to record much minutiae which may or may not turn out to be useful in future research. In a true inductive science, observation must precede synthesis and the intensive mining of limited sectors of experience becomes a necessary precondition for the development of theory. We take comfort, in this document, in Homan's declaration that "a case method means, in the first place, that general theories are shown to arise out of, and be supported by, specific, detailed, matters of observation."[22]

We are further consoled by the same author's willingness to forgive his own imperfections. "Nothing we have said already, or will say hereafter, can be taken to imply that this book tells the whole story about the group, or anything like the whole story. It will be incomplete partly by reason of human frailty and partly by design. In any event it will be incomplete, but incompleteness may be creative, if one man's lack becomes another's incentive."[23]

The Sober Alcoholic

Historical Development of Alcoholics Anonymous[1]

The beginnings of Alcoholics Anonymous can be traced back to the summer of 1934 when Bill W., founder of A.A. was a patient in Town's Hospital in New York City. This was just another in a long series of hospitalizations for Bill. His doctor, William Silkworth, had just diagnosed the case as hopeless alcoholism. It was at this point that Bill W. reports a "spiritual" revelation.

> My depression deepened unbearably and finally it seemed to me as though I were at the very bottom of a pit. All at once I found myself crying out, "If there is a God, let Him show Himself! I am ready to do anything!" Suddenly the room lit up with a great white light. I was caught up into an ecstasy which there are no words to describe. It seemed to me, in the mind's eye, that I was on a mountain and that a wind not of air but of spirit was blowing. And then it burst upon me that I was a free man. Slowly the ecstasy subsided. I lay on the bed, but now for a time I was in another world, a new world of consciousness. All about me and through me there was a feeling of Presence, and I thought to myself, "So this is the God of the Preachers!" A great peace stole over me and I thought, "No matter how wrong things seem to be they are still alright. Things are alright with God and His world."[2]

This experience has become part of the basic tradition of Alcoholics Anonymous and is acknowledged by other members who consider the achievement of sobriety a "spiritual awakening." At first Bill thought he was having hallucinations, but Dr.

Silkworth assured him that this was a form of emotional release which sometimes frees people from the alcoholic compulsion.

As soon as he was discharged from the hospital Bill affiliated himself with the Oxford Group Movement, a religious revivalist organization founded by Dr. Frank N. Buchman, a Lutheran minister from Pennsylvania. Bill was referred to the Oxford Group by a longtime friend and drinking companion, Ebby. Ebby, also a hopeless alcoholic, had achieved sobriety, at least temporarily, through association with the Oxford Group. Ebby told Bill, "I learned that I had to admit I was licked; I learned that I had to take stock of myself and confess my defects to another person in confidence; I learned that I needed to make restitution for the harm I had done others."[3] These precepts were part of the Oxford Group doctrine and ultimately were incorporated into the A.A. program. The contribution made by the Oxford Group to the development of A.A. is discussed in more detail in a later chapter dealing with A.A. as a religious movement.

Bill W. hoped that through the Oxford Group he would be most effective in helping other alcoholics, even though the Group had had almost no success in solving this particular problem. Several members even discouraged him from continuing in what they considered to be a hopeless cause.

At this point, in May, 1935, Bill went to Akron, Ohio on a business trip. The enterprise collapsed and Bill found himself stranded, alone and without funds, in Akron. He remembered that when he was most depressed he usually felt better if he was able to discuss his problems with some other alcoholic. The question was where to find one with whom he could talk in this strange town. He called a member of the Oxford Group who finally put him in touch with another alcoholic, Dr. Bob, the co-founder of A.A. Their initial discussion proved beneficial to both men—and the practice of one alcoholic talking to another became a fundamental part of A.A. therapy.

Bill and Dr. Bob then decided to broaden their efforts to try to help other alcoholics in Akron. They had one success at the Akron City Hospital where Bill D., the third member of

A.A., joined forces with them. Additional attempts to help others met with failure, thus limiting the nucleus of A.A. to these three members.

Bill then returned to New York City and began to form another small group of recovered alcoholics. By the fall of 1935 a core of members had been established. These activities were carried out while Bill still remained affiliated with the Oxford Group Movement. However, it was becoming increasingly apparent that the principal goals of the two organizations were incompatible and that a break would have to come sooner or later.

The Oxford Group intended to save the world, whereas Bill and his group wanted only to help as many alcoholics as possible. The Oxford's concepts of Absolute Purity, Absolute Honesty, Absolute Unselfishness, and Absolute Love were difficult for most alcoholics to comprehend, let alone to achieve. There was a still more important reason for the dissolution of the association with the Oxford people. Because of the stigma attached to being an alcoholic it was not at all advantageous for problem drinkers to publicize the fact that they had joined a group to help them overcome this affliction. Anonymity was impossible in the Oxford Group which relied heavily on the use of prominent names to attract additional members. Obviously some other format was needed to protect the privacy of alcoholics. Thus, in the fall of 1937, the alcoholics disassociated themselves from the Oxford Group Movement, although they borrowed considerably from the principles and practices of Buchman's followers.

Gradually the New York and Akron groups began to increase in size. Bill paid another visit to Akron in the latter part of 1937 and met with Dr. Bob to review what had transpired since their first meeting. There was now a solid nucleus of over thirty recovered alcoholics in New York and Akron. Apparently the program had considerable merit, and plans had to be made to broaden and intensify their efforts. It was decided to embark on a campaign to publicize the activities of this new fellowship which was as yet unnamed. In addition it was suggested that the methods and philosophies of this new movement be recorded in writing so that they could be more readily available to larger numbers of people. For this purpose it was finally agreed that a book should be published which would include the principles and techniques of recovery. This would also prevent distortion of the original group philosophies.

The idea to publish a book met with strong opposition from some of the members but they were finally won over. The problem now remained to obtain financial backing for this project and for the promotion of the program. It was not anticipated that this would be too difficult in view of the preliminary success that they had achieved and the importance of the problem of alcoholism.

Bill returned to New York in a rather optimistic frame of mind, ready to launch the campaign. However, he was dismayed to discover that the wealthy people who he had anticipated would be delighted to sponsor the project rejected the idea entirely. Why, they felt, should they contribute money to an unheard of group of alcoholics when there were many respectable and established causes appealing for their funds?

After nearly exhausting all possibilities, Bill arranged an appointment to see Willard Richardson, manager of John D. Rockefeller, Jr.'s donations to private charities. Richardson indicated his interest and Bill was exuberant. A second meeting was tentatively arranged to be attended by a small number of influential friends of Mr. Richardson. Dr. Bob and Bill W. would have this opportunity to state their case in full. This meeting was held in December, 1937. It was decided that an investigation of the movement was warranted prior to an official request to Mr. Rockefeller for financial assistance. This was done and a favorable report was submitted. To the utter disappointment of Bill and the others, Rockefeller turned down the request for funds although he highly commended the aims and purposes of the group.

At the time, Bill thought that this was the final blow, but it turned out to be a significant turning point which was to establish the future financial policy of A.A. Rockefeller said he firmly believed that a large grant of money at that time would have ruined the movement rather than have helped it. He felt that the problems associated with handling large sums of money would have presented some serious hazards to the ultimate success of the group. However, he did place the sum of $5,000 in trust for temporary relief of the immediate problems of Bill and Dr. Bob, who were both bankrupt. In addition Rockefeller suggested that the group become financially independent so that they would not be subject to pressure from outside sources. This became the firm policy of A.A. and is strongly adhered to today. Not only did it turn out to be a good monetary policy, but it became an effective part of the rehabilitative process because these alcoholics, who were formerly irresponsible, to say the least, were now relying on themselves and were proud of the fact that they were able to decline outside financial assistance. For people who formerly begged, borrowed, and stole for a drink, it is not difficult to see the therapeutic support derived from this form of economic maturity. At this earlier date, however, they still felt a dire need for money and continued their fund-raising efforts.

In the spring of 1938 it was decided that some kind of formal organization was needed to unify the rather amorphous movement. It was suggested that the recovered alcoholics establish a foundation which would be tax free and to which wealthy persons could make contributions with a greater feeling of security.

This was the first step in forming the Alcoholic Foundation, since renamed the General Service Board of Alcoholics Anonymous. The first meeting of the newly created Alcoholic Foundation was held in May, 1938, and a Board of Trustees consisting of three non-alcoholics and two alcoholics was established. At that time it was decided that the alcoholic members of the Board would always be a minority by a margin of one, but in 1959 equal representation was instituted. It was felt that in the early formative days the control of the organization should be vested in the non-alcoholic majority, but such a safeguard is not currently required.

In the spring of 1938, Bill began work on the book of A.A. principles and history. A publisher was interested and agreed to advance $1,500, the amount to be deducted from future royalties. However, Bill decided that it would be better for the Foundation if it retained complete control by publishing the book itself. The trustees in the Foundation did not approve of this idea but Bill went ahead despite their lack of support. A separate unit called Works Publishing, Inc. was formed. The proposed six hundred shares of stock in Works Publishing, Inc. did not sell at all until the *Readers Digest* expressed interest in the book and the movement. With this encouraging news, stock in the amount of $5,000 was finally sold. Bill was thus able to continue work on the book which was due to be completed in April, 1939. In December, 1938, the Twelve Steps of Alcoholics Anonymous were formulated and incorporated into the A.A. book as guiding principles.[4]

THE TWELVE STEPS

STEP ONE: We admitted that we were powerless over alcohol—that our lives had become unmanageable.

STEP TWO: Came to believe that a Power greater than ourselves could restore us to sanity.

STEP THREE: Made a decision to turn our will and our lives over to the care of God as we understood Him.

STEP FOUR: Made a searching and fearless moral inventory of ourselves.

STEP FIVE: Admitted to God, to ourselves, and to another human being the exact nature of our wrongs.

STEP SIX: Were entirely ready to have God remove all these defects of character.

STEP SEVEN: Humbly asked Him to remove our shortcomings.

STEP EIGHT: Made a list of all persons we had harmed and became willing to make amends to them all.

STEP NINE: Made direct amends to such people when-
                 ever possible, except when to do so would
                 injure them or others.

STEP TEN: Continued to take personal inventory and
                 when we were wrong promptly admitted it.

STEP ELEVEN: Sought through prayer and meditation to
                 improve our conscious contact with God as
                 we understood Him, praying only for knowl-
                 edge of His will for us and the power to
                 carry that out.

STEP TWELVE: Having had a spiritual awakening as a result
                 of these steps, we tried to practice these prin-
                 ciples in all our affairs.

Considerable debate and controversy arose when Bill first
discussed these steps with the other group members. It was
ultimately agreed that the steps should be included in the book
in their original form.

The first suggested title for the book was *Alcoholics Anonymous* stemming from the early days in which Bill described
himself and his associates as "a shameless bunch of alcoholics."
However, the title *The Way Out* was also popular with many
of the members. Research indicated that the Library of Congress already had twelve books titled *The Way Out* and not
a single book titled *Alcoholics Anonymous*. Thus *Alcoholics
Anonymous* was approved and sent to the printer.[5]

With the establishment of the Foundation, and with a list
of wealthy potential contributors to be solicited, it was thought
that the financial problems of the group would soon be solved.
However, the contributions did not materialize and the Foundation remained as impoverished as ever. To make matters worse,
the *Readers Digest*, which had formerly indicated its willingness to publicize the book, now stated that it could not, or
would not, be able to implement such a plan because of the
sensitive nature of the subject of alcoholism.

Nevertheless, *Alcoholics Anonymous*, which also became the
name of the group, was published in 1939 and was favorably

reviewed by Dr. Harry Emerson Fosdick. Despite the fact that this review was printed in many religious periodicals and that the New York *Times* also published a brief report, only a handful of orders for the book was received and the financial situation remained as desperate as ever. Gabriel Heatter interviewed a member of the group on his nationwide radio program but interest in the movement still remained dormant. Eventually, a certain amount of activity became discernible.

Fulton Oursler, then editor of *Liberty* magazine, agreed to publish a feature article on Alcoholics Anonymous. The report, titled "Alcoholics and God," appeared in September, 1939, and resulted in about eight hundred requests for help, all of which were turned over to A.A. A personal letter from the group was sent to each inquirer and several hundred books were sold in this fashion. This was the first mark of progress in reaching the public.

At this time the Cleveland *Plain Dealer* ran a series of articles about A.A. which resulted in a veritable deluge of requests for more information. A.A. groups were formed in Cleveland in June, 1939, and membership grew rapidly. Within twelve months there were over twenty-five groups with several hundred members in the Cleveland area. By early 1940 it was estimated that there were about eight hundred recovered alcoholics in the movement throughout the United States.

In 1940 the first A.A. clubhouse was opened at 334½ West 24th Street, New York City. The building has become an A.A. shrine. When the entire area was condemned to make way for a new housing project in 1959, the clubhouse was disasssembled and restored at a new location on 23rd Street in New York City.

In the spring of 1940 the A.A. office, by dint of the increasing volume of correspondence, was forced to move from its small quarters in Newark to a larger space at 30 Vesey Street in Manhattan. The amount of mail received from all parts of the country mounted. Bill and one underpaid, overworked secretary found it impossible to answer all the inquiries.

Interest in A.A. was further stimulated by a dinner sponsored by John D. Rockefeller, Jr., and held at the Union Club on

February 8, 1940. Rockefeller had maintained his interest in A.A. and felt that he could now help with some constructive action. He proposed a dinner meeting to which he would invite some of his influential friends. Four hundred invitations were sent out and seventy-five people attended. Rockefeller himself was taken ill, and his son, Nelson, presided over the affair. Much to the utter dismay of the A.A. members, Nelson Rockefeller did not solicit funds but rather made the following statement, "Gentlemen, you can all see that this is a work of goodwill. Its power lies in the fact that one member carries the good message to the next, without any thought of financial income or reward. Therefore, it is our belief that Alcoholics Anonymous should be self-supporting so far as money is concerned. It needs only our goodwill."[6]

With this the dinner concluded, and the guests, representing hundreds of millions of dollars, walked out. However, Rockefeller dispatched a personal letter to those who had attended the meeting reiterating his faith in A.A. He indicated that despite the need for financial independence a little temporary help might be advisable and stated that he was donating the modest sum of $1,000. An additional $2,000 was collected in the form of small donations from these people. Far more important than the monetary support was the favorable publicity which followed.

In 1940 the Alcoholic Foundation took over the stock of Works Publishing, Inc., the organization which had been established for the purpose of publishing the "Big Book,"[7] *Alcoholics Anonymous*. The entire organization became more stable and a solid foundation for growth and expansion was established. Local A.A. groups were forming in most major cities and by early 1941 the membership figure had risen to an estimated two thousand.

The biggest impetus to A.A. growth was still to come. On March 1, 1941, an article about A.A. by Jack Alexander was published in the *Saturday Evening Post*. The A.A. office was immediately deluged with pleas for help, inquiries for more information, and orders for the book *Alcoholics Anonymous*. The volunteers who staffed the office were unable to keep up with the volume of work and two regular paid employees were hired.

At the end of 1941 membership was estimated at eight thousand, an increase of six thousand in one year.

This growth was accompanied by new problems. Some of the new members felt they had discovered a marketable commodity, and attempts were made to commercialize A.A. therapy. A vicious rumor circulated to the effect that the Foundation was just a device which Bill was using to enrich himself. It was even reported that Bill and Dr. Bob were dividing $64,000 annually between them, this money being supplied by Rockefeller. Additionally there were a number of cases in which entire groups strayed from sobriety, hardly an endorsement for the program.

Actually Bill and Dr. Bob were far from affluent. Dr. Bob was receiving $30.00 per week from the Rockefeller fund, as was Bill. Bill received an additional $25.00 per week as royalties from sales of the "Big Book." The Foundation itself was still virtually bankrupt. All funds received were desperately needed to keep the office in operation.

In 1942 the Serenity Prayer was adopted for use by A.A. The origin of this prayer is uncertain, but it was seen by an A.A. member in a New York newspaper, was reprinted on small cards, and was included with all mail sent out of the A.A. office. The prayer itself, conspicuously exhibited at all meetings, is also referred to as an important therapeutic support.

God grant me the serenity to accept the things I cannot change, courage to change the things I can, and the wisdom to know the difference.

With the continued growth of A.A., additional office space was needed and another move was made to larger quarters at 415 Lexington Avenue, in New York City. The scope of A.A. activities had burst the national boundary and communications poured in from all parts of the world. Sales of the "Big Book" increased and a variety of brochures were printed, each dealing with a different aspect of the alcoholic problem.

In 1944 a monthly periodical called the A.A. *Grapevine* was published and remains today as the official journal of Alcoholics

Anonymous.[8] Circulation is also international. The editor, editorial board, artists, and writers are all unpaid volunteers.

The Traditions of Alcoholics Anonymous were first published in the *A.A. Grapevine* on May 6, 1946. These Traditions are now incorporated in a separate volume and represent the "formal" guide for individual and group activity.[9]

The summer of 1950 marked the first international convention of A.A., held in Cleveland, Ohio and attended by three thousand members. The Twelve Traditions were confirmed at the convention as the permanent guiding principles of Alcoholics Anonymous. During this year the Headquarters expanded still further and moved to 141 East 44th Street, New York City.

Also in this year Bill started to think about a world-wide conference of A.A. delegates to link all local group activities into some common unit with the Alcoholic Foundation. The Trustees approved the conference plan and the first General Service Conference met in New York City in April, 1951. The Conference suggested that the Alcoholic Foundation be renamed the General Service Board of Alcoholics Anonymous. It was not until two years later that this was actually put into effect.

In 1951, A.A. was awarded the Lasker Award by the American Public Health Association. In 1953, a book-length interpretation of A.A. principles by co-founder Bill W. was published under the title *Twelve Steps and Twelve Traditions*. This is a small text which explains the basic tenets and their application in the A.A. program.

In July, 1955, Alcoholics Anonymous held a twentieth anniversary convention in St. Louis, attended by over five thousand members and friends. It was also at this time that the "Big Book" *Alcoholics Anonymous* was revised and expanded in a second edition.[10]

The twenty-fifth anniversary convention of Alcoholics Anonymous was held in San Francisco in 1960. As an indication of the continued growth of the fellowship, on September 4, 1962, the General Service Board of A.A. announced a count of 9,305 active groups, a figure double that of ten years earlier.

As Alcoholics Anonymous established itself as a favorable force in providing help for the alcoholic, family members of problem drinkers sought a similar solution for coping with their own distress. Two organizations have sprung up to furnish these individuals with some means of dealing with the impact of alcoholism on their own lives. These associations are the Al-Anon Family Groups for adult relatives and friends of problem drinkers and the Alateen program for children whose parents are alcoholics. Although not officially affiliated with Alcoholics Anonymous these organizations are the offspring of A.A. and closely resemble it in format and procedures.

The emergence of these two associations demonstrates the widespread effect, and in essence an unanticipated consequence, of the A.A. movement. It is not our purpose to offer a detailed account here of the systems of Al-Anon and Alateen. For those interested a description of the two associations appears in the appendix in this volume.

CHAPTER TWO

The Formal Structure of the National Organization

THE GENERAL SERVICE BOARD OF ALCOHOLICS ANONYMOUS

Organized in 1938 as the Alcoholic Foundation, the General Service Board of Alcoholics Anonymous is also the Board of Trustees and is in effect the international service agency of Alcoholics Anonymous. There are currently sixteen members on the Board—eight non-alcoholics and eight alcoholics. All are elected to the Board and serve without compensation. The alcoholic members may hold office for a maximum of four years while the non-alcoholic officers may serve indefinitely.

The Board is responsible for domestic and world-wide public relations, maintains the A.A. Traditions, and oversees A.A. operating funds. It also safeguards the standards of the Alcoholics Anonymous Publishing, Inc. and the A.A. Grapevine, Inc.

THE GENERAL SERVICE HEADQUARTERS OF ALCOHOLICS ANONYMOUS

The General Service Headquarters is responsible for the day-to-day service operations under the Board's guidance. It corresponds with people seeking help and with new and established groups. It handles inquiries from the general public and representatives of industry, medicine, and religion. General Service coordinates activities with radio, press, television, and film producers. It communicates with Loners,[1] institutional and overseas groups.

The General Service Headquarters also issues a Directory listing A.A. groups throughout the world. This Directory is published annually and is used extensively by A.A. members who may be traveling to different states or countries and may want to attend meetings or to make local contacts.

Headquarters attends to all details of the annual General Service Conference which brings together representatives of the movement to review the work of the service agencies and to advise on future activities. Correspondence is maintained with groups and individuals in approximately fifty countries. Foreign language translations of A.A. literature are also distributed.

ALCOHOLICS ANONYMOUS PUBLISHING, INC.

Originally created by the A.A. founders as a means of publishing the "Big Book" *Alcoholics Anonymous*,[2] Alcoholics Anonymous Publishing, Inc., is now the exclusive agency of the association. This company handles the printing and distribution of A.A.'s basic texts—*Alcoholics Anonymous, Twelve Steps and Twelve Traditions*, and *A.A. Comes of Age*. It also issues the long list of pamphlet literature available to all A.A. local groups at a nominal price.[3] Local groups distribute the pamphlets free to members and newcomers.

Net income derived from the sale of A.A. literature is used mainly to create a reserve fund to assure continuation of worldwide service in case of a period of economic hardship. The General Service Board also has granted Bill W., as the surviving co-founder of the movement, a fifteen per cent royalty on sales of A.A. books. These royalties represent Bill's only income from A.A. sources.

THE ALCOHOLICS ANONYMOUS GRAPEVINE, INC.

This corporation is responsible for the preparation and distribution of a pocket-size magazine which is represented as the international monthly journal of Alcoholics Anonymous. A typical issue will contain approximately fifteen two- or three-page articles by members of A.A. throughout the world. These are usually concerned with the personal experiences and opinions of the writers. Cartoons and illustrations by members are also included. In addition the publication devotes a small section to activities and developments in the field of alcoholism outside of A.A. All contributions are submitted without remuneration.

Although the General Service Board has responsibility for the general integrity of the journal, control of editorial policy is vested in its Board of Directors. If the subscriber is sensitive about maintaining anonymity, the *Grapevine* is mailed in a first-class sealed envelope at an additional $1.50 per year. Some local groups obtain a multiple subscription at a slightly reduced rate which provides them with a small profit when resold to members at thirty-five cents a copy.

THE GENERAL SERVICE CONFERENCE

Established in 1951, the General Service Conference is the link between local A.A. groups and the structural hierarchy. The Conference meets annually in April in New York City. Each A.A. group has a General Service representative who meets with other representatives at certain cities in their respective states. These meetings are called Group Assemblies the purpose of which is to elect delegates to the General Service Conference. The delegates are elected for two-year terms. Each state is allowed one delegate, but where A.A. membership is extremely heavy, extra representation is provided. A special seventy-page booklet titled *The Third Legacy Manual of A.A. World Service,*[4] published in 1955, discusses the formation of the Conference, the function of the Conference, and spells out in detail the Conference Charter. In general the Conference receives and evaluates reports on A.A. national and international service facilities, discusses matters of general A.A. interest, and advises the Board of Trustees on the best means of fulfilling A.A. policy. The Conference acts solely in an advisory capacity and has no formal authority to regulate the fellowship.

THE INTERGROUP ASSOCIATION OF ALCOHOLICS ANONYMOUS

The Intergroup Association is the New York metropolitan area coordinating office and communications center. It is located at 133 East 39th Street, and has a street-level office with a small sign on the outer entrance. Intergroup is supported by contributions from metropolitan area groups. Most groups pledge a certain amount to Intergroup each month, but some groups with limited resources contribute very little, if at all. If a regularly contributing group should neglect its donation, a short reminder will be sent from Intergroup concerning the oversight. No fixed amount is set by A.A. or by Intergroup; each group contributes what it can afford.

Each local group elects a delegate and an alternate to Intergroup semi-annually. The delegates meet at least twice during this six-month period. They are responsible for the election of the Intergroup Steering Committee and officers. The Steering Committee meets once a month to take action on matters of policy.

The Association employs one part-time and two full-time secretaries. Much of the contact work is carried on by volunteer members of A.A. The Intergroup office is the reception center for local calls from people asking for assistance. Seven or eight volunteers are on duty every day, including Sundays and holidays, to answer these calls and to make the necessary arrangements for the alcoholic seeking help.

These volunteers work at individual desks equipped with a telephone and a large loose-leaf binder which is a directory of all groups in the metropolitan area, listing the group name, address, time of meetings, group officers, and members available for Twelfth Step work. When an incoming call is received, the A.A. member answering asks the caller if he wants help. In all cases the caller or his representative must assure the A.A. member that he is personally seeking assistance. If this is the case the A.A. member obtains the name and address of the person calling.

If the caller is obviously too inebriated to be coherent no further action is taken. The same applies to calls originating from bars or cocktail lounges. If the caller appears to be sincere and is in a place where he can be reached, he is advised that some members of a local group close to his place of residence will contact him as soon as possible. On occasion the caller prefers to be contacted by a group from a different area because he feels that he may know some of the people in the neighborhood nearest to him and this might be embarrassing. The A.A. member will complete the necessary arrangements. He will refer to the directory and call the local group secretary or one of the other officers or people listed as available for Twelfth Step work. The local group will then have two of its members call on the alcoholic seeking help. They will usually take him to a meeting that same night. More serious cases may be hospitalized in one of the special institutions which accepts A.A. referrals.

People also come directly to the Intergroup office, looking for assistance. In such cases the A.A. member will discuss this person's problem with him at great length if so desired. The individual may also be given A.A. literature and a meeting list of all groups in the metropolitan area with certain suggestions about which one might be most convenient for him.

Three or four active alcoholics may always be found in the Intergroup office sitting in the "back room"—which is sort of an informal "drying out" place. This affords some of these active drinkers a haven for the day and the possibility that they may be helped by being in close proximity to A.A.

During a typical day the office handles one hundred incoming calls, makes about sixty outgoing calls, and receives about forty personal visitors. A follow-up form is filled out in duplicate when a caller is referred to a local group. One copy of this form is kept in the Intergroup files and the other is sent to the local group secretary. The form contains the names of the person who called and the member of the local group to whom the caller was referred. By such means the group is able to keep a record of which members are handling most of the Twelfth Step contacts with Intergroup.

The Intergroup office also acts as the referral center for those alcoholics who need hospitalization. Most cases are sent to Town's Hospital, a small private institution on Central Park West. Here the alcoholic will be hospitalized for five days at a cost of ninety dollars. He will be under medical supervision and will also be visited by A.A. members. Meetings are held daily in the ward. An informal social structure is established within the hospital. One patient is "elected" as "mayor" of the ward and acts as unofficial assistant to the nurse in charge. He is also in charge of the "kitty" to which each patient contributes five dollars when he enters Town's and which pays for cigarettes, soft drinks, and snacks ordered from outside. Because a man will not become "mayor" until he shows physical and emotional improvement (usually the third day, and he only stays five), the position changes hands frequently.

Other important functions of Intergroup:

1. Periodically compiles, revises, and distributes the A.A. meeting list as well as a small booklet titled, *An Introduction to A.A.*

2. Distributes a list of names, addresses, and telephone numbers of secretaries and program chairmen of all A.A. groups.

3. Conducts the program exchange meeting every three months.

4. In January and July of each year conducts a "get acquainted" meeting for new secretaries and other officers.

5. Arranges an annual A.A. dinner to celebrate Bill W.'s anniversary. Proceeds after expenses help support the Intergroup office.

6. Furnishes volunteers for a variety of public relations activities—radio, television, churches, colleges.

7. Arranges for quarterly institutions representatives' meeting and distributes a monthly Institutions Bulletin.

8. Prints and distributes a weekly "bulletin" which goes to all groups and includes items and notes of interest to members.

GENERAL POLICY OF ALCOHOLICS ANONYMOUS

Financial Policy

The world-wide program of Alcoholics Anonymous is supported by voluntary contributions from local groups, donations by individual members directly to General Service Headquarters, and funds derived from various publishing activities. Individual donations may not exceed $100 a year. Group contributions are made on the suggested basis of $3.00 per year per member.

A.A. accounts are audited and financial statements are issued annually. The writer has seen these audit reports and can confirm that they are complete in every detail in accordance with good business practice.

A.A. *Objectives*

The objectives of Alcoholics Anonymous are summed up in the following passage called the A.A. Preamble which is printed on the inside cover of most A.A. publications. It is read by the group chairman at the commencement of all meetings.

> Alcoholics Anonymous is a fellowship of men and women who share their experience, strength and hope with each other that they may solve their common problem and help others to recover from alcoholism.
>
> The only requirement for membership is a desire to stop drinking. There are no dues or fees for A.A. membership; we are self-supporting through our own contributions. A.A. is not allied with any sect, denomination, politics, organization or institution; does not wish to engage in any controversy; neither endorses nor opposes any causes. Our primary purpose is to stay sober and help other alcoholics to achieve sobriety.

This statement clearly defines the purpose of the association. Alcoholics Anonymous does not engage in, or finance, research in alcoholism. It does not maintain or support hospitals, clinics, or rest homes although there is an unofficial affiliation with some treatment and recovery facilities. For instance, Intergroup Association refers all alcoholics in need of hospitalization to Town's Hospital in New York City where one floor is devoted to treatment of A.A. alcoholics. There is also an excellent special hospital in Paterson, New Jersey, called Mt. Carmel. Other recuperation homes are scattered throughout the metropolitan area. A.A. does not support these institutions in any way except to refer patients to them.

A.A. takes no official position on temperance and has never affiliated itself with any public or private effort to enact prohibition. Members of A.A. as individuals serve on paid staffs of institutions and foundations investigating the problems of alcoholism. In such cases the individual is not employed as, and does not indicate that he is, a representative of Alcoholics Anonymous. Cooperation is also extended to valid professional and business organizations expressing interest in A.A. techniques. In no case, however, does A.A. lend its official endorsement to any causes outside its own sphere.

A.A. Traditions

In addition to the objectives outlined above, a set of principles to guide group activity has been documented.[5] These Twelve Traditions are not official rules or regulations but they do provide direction and guidance for group action and for the proper resolution of problems which may arise.

TRADITION ONE: "Our common welfare should come first; personal recovery depends upon A.A. unity."[6]

Although A.A. stresses the welfare of the individual, it could not be of service if group unity and cohesion should be fragmented. Individual problems must be subordinate to the continuity of the group. Obviously the group must survive or the individual will not.

TRADITION TWO: "For our group purpose there is but one ultimate authority—a loving God as He may express Himself in our group conscience. Our leaders are but trusted servants; they do not govern."[7]

This tradition refers to the theoretical lack of leadership in A.A. and points to the concept that the "group conscience" is actually the prime guiding force. Leadership in local groups is rotated every six months, and one often hears that officers are not to "run things" but are to serve as instruments for the expression of the collective will.

TRADITION THREE: "The only requirement for A.A. membership is a desire to stop drinking."[8]

This is certainly unique to Alcoholics Anonymous—"You are an A.A. member if you say so. No matter what you have done, or still will do, you are an A.A. member as long as you say so."[9] The absolute self-determination of membership with no formal mechanism for expelling a self-defined member is a distinguishing characteristic of the fellowship. Social control in such a permissive milieu obviously presents some interesting problems which are discussed in detail in a later chapter. Suffice it to say at this point that no person may be excluded from affiliation if he expresses a desire to stop drinking nor can he be ousted for any form of deviant behavior.

TRADITION FOUR: "Each group should be autonomous, except in matters affecting other groups or A.A. as a whole."[10]

This tradition indicates the nature of the organizational structure in A.A. in which authority stems from the local group and extends upward to the service units. "This sort of liberty prevents A.A. from becoming a frozen set of dogmatic principles that could not be changed even when obviously wrong. Of course any dissident group is urged—though never commanded —not to make any other affiliation. An A.A. group should not ally itself with any particular brand of medicine or psychiatric treatment. We can cooperate with anyone. But the name 'Alcoholics Anonymous' must be reserved for us only."[11]

"We obey these principles because we think they are good principles. At the final end of obedience we obey A.A.'s Steps and Traditions because we really want them for ourselves. It is no longer a question of good or evil; we conform because we genuinely want to conform."[12]

TRADITION FIVE: "Each group has but one primary purpose —to carry its message to the alcoholic who still suffers."[13]

Because there are countless alcoholics still in need of help, and with no relief in sight, the objectives of A.A. will never be fully realized. As long as there is no cure for alcoholism and members must maintain their affiliation with A.A. to keep sober, there is little likelihood of the disintegration of the association because of a lack of need.

TRADITION SIX: "An A.A. group ought never to endorse, finance, or lend the A.A. name to any related facility or outside enterprise, lest problems of money, property, and prestige divert us from our primary purpose."[14]

In the early days of A.A. it was felt that the organization could be a vital force in education, research, politics, and even world affairs. It became evident that by adhering to its primary purpose, and by not becoming involved in outside affairs, its chances of success would be considerably improved. This philosophy of non-involvement also meant that A.A. would not require large expenditures of funds. Staying sober and helping others to do so require minimum financing.

"It is in this sense that A.A. has declared for the principle of corporate poverty."[15] This is another unique characteristic of A.A. which differentiates it from other national voluntary organizations. No fund drives and no solicitation campaigns on behalf of A.A. are ever undertaken. This establishes two major advantages. The fact that these recovered alcoholics do not need and do not want financial assistance from outside sources is an important element in promoting favorable public relations. Secondly, for the member of A.A. there is great satisfaction in being self-sufficient. Many of these people were financially insolvent and poor credit risks. Now they belong to an organization which declines offers of monetary aid.

TRADITION SEVEN: "Every A.A. group ought to be fully self-supporting, declining outside contributions."[16]

This is an outgrowth of the circumstances described in Tradition Six. In addition, each A.A. local group is financially independent. Although some groups are literally without funds and others are affluent, there is no borrowing by one group from another.

TRADITION EIGHT: "Alcoholics Anonymous should remain forever non-professional, but our service centers may employ special workers."[17]

No professional therapists operate within A.A. circles nor does any A.A. member charge for his service in the program. It is true that some A.A. members are involved in various activities in the field of alcoholism for which they do receive payment but such full-time careers are hardly exploitation of A.A. for monetary gain.

TRADITION NINE: "A.A., as such, ought never to be organized, but we may create service boards or committees directly responsible to those they serve."[18]

What we really mean, of course, is that A.A. can never have an organized direction or government. To amplify this: Did anyone ever hear of a nation, a church, a political party, even a benevolent association that had no membership rules? Did anyone ever hear of a society that could not somehow discipline its members and enforce obedience to necessary rules and regulations? Does not nearly every society on earth give authority to some of its members to impose obedience upon the rest and to punish or expel offenders? Power to direct and to govern is the essence of organization.

To this rule Alcoholics Anonymous is a complete exception. It does not at any point conform to the pattern of a government. Neither its General Service Conference, its General Service Board nor the humblest group committee can issue a single directive to an A.A. member and make it stick let alone hand out any punishment. An A.A. member may take advice or suggestions from more experienced members but surely he will not take orders.[19]

Social control is of course a strong force in maintaining order. No organization of any kind could exist if each individual member had as much actual freedom as implied above. This will be analyzed in more detail in our review, later, of the system of social control in the local group.

TRADITION TEN: "Alcoholics Anonymous has no opinion on outside issues; hence the A.A. name ought never be drawn into public controversy."[20]

Alcoholics Anonymous benefited from the experience of the Washington Movement which had an auspicious beginning in Baltimore in 1840.[21] The Movement was initiated by a small number of alcoholics and within a matter of months had built up a tremendous following. Within two years it spread beyond the Alleghenies into the new states of the Middle West. Its membership reached a high of 500,000. However, it became embroiled in a variety of political matters and extended itself far beyond the scope of the basic problem of the alcoholic. The rising opposition of political, church, and temperance leaders brought about the gradual disappearance of the Movement. A.A. is firmly convinced that it will avoid any such complications by rigidly adhering to its basic principles, and by not becoming involved in extraneous issues.

At one time it was thought that A.A. might obtain a Congressional Charter through an act of the United States Congress, which would afford it some legal protection and put it on the same plane as the American Red Cross and similar national associations. However, it was finally decided not to seek such a charter for the following reasons:

1. A Congressional incorporation would create by law a power to govern which would be contrary to, and violative of, our Traditions.
2. When we ask for legal rights, enforceable in courts of law, we by the same act subject ourselves to possible legal regulation.
3. We might become endlessly entangled in litigation which, together with the incidental expense and publicity, could seriously threaten our very existence.
4. Incorporation of A.A. could conceivably become the opening wedge that might engender politics and a struggle for power within our own ranks.
5. Continuously since its beginning, and today, A.A. has been a fellowship and not an organization. Incorporation necessarily makes it an organization.
6. We believe that "spiritual faith" and a "way of life" cannot be incorporated.[22]

TRADITION ELEVEN: "Our public relations policy is based on attraction rather than promotion; we need always maintain personal anonymity at the level of press, radio, films and television."[23]

This is directly contrary to the policy of almost all other voluntary associations which fully exploit their "big names" for purposes of fund raising and membership recruiting. In A.A. personal publicity has yielded to group public relations resulting in a highly favorable response from the mass media and from the general population.

The 1956 General Service Conference of A.A. adopted the following statement of "A.A.'s Movement-Wide Public Information Policy":

> In all public relationships, A.A.'s sole objective is to help the still suffering alcoholic. Always mindful of the importance of personal anonymity, we believe this can be done by making known to him, and to those who may be interested in his problem our own experience as individuals and as a fellowship in learning to live without alcohol.
>
> We believe that our experience should be made available freely to all who express sincere interest. We believe further that all our efforts in this field should always reflect our gratitude for the gift of sobriety and our awareness that many outside A.A. are equally concerned with the serious problem of alcoholism.[24]

TRADITION TWELVE: "Anonymity is the spiritual foundation of our tradition, ever reminding us to place principles before personalities."[25]

Anonymity provides for the protection of members within the association who would prefer that others did not know of their being alcoholics. Simultaneously it protects the unity and strength of the organization. If no individual is identified as a member, then should this person "slip" or get drunk it will not reflect negatively on A.A.

This survey of the national organization provides a general perspective of the structural components, the communication pattern, the program's objectives and the overall normative system. The major concern has not been with individuals but rather with broad organizational functions.

The succeeding chapters deal more explicitly with the "bonds of organization," focusing on the local unit as typified by the East End group.

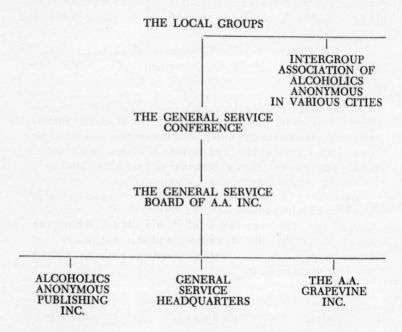

FIGURE 1. *Elements in the Formal Structure of the National Organization*

CHAPTER THREE

The Formal Structure of the East End Group of A.A.

The formal organization of the East End group consists of the following elements:

1. Steering Committee
2. Chairman
3. Treasurer
4. Secretary
5. Program Chairman
6. Intergroup Delegate and Alternate
7. Institutions Representative
8. General Service Representative

All officers are elected for a term of six months. The officers are nominated by a special committee appointed by the chairman, consisting of three "older" group members who are acquainted with the entire membership. Invariably only one slate of officers is nominated and even this is sometimes difficult to complete. No officer is allowed to succeed himself or hold the same office until a two-year period has elapsed. Because the total membership usually does not exceed thirty people it is sometimes difficult to pick a complete and competent slate of officers. To compensate for this, an officer can be selected for a position other than the one he has held for the preceding six months. Thus a treasurer in one term may be elected chairman for the following administration. This actually was the case when Bob R. was treasurer from June 15th to December 15th and was then elected chairman.

The election takes place during a special business meeting which precedes the regular closed session the week prior to the actual date of installation. The voting is purely a formality because there is never more than one slate selected and accepted unanimously. There are no voting requirements except presumed membership in the group. Ballots are not secret and a hand count determines the result.

There are no restrictions or special qualifications for an officer except that the member must have a minimum of three months sobriety. The chairman may be male or female but preference is given to a male. Likewise the secretary may be male or female but a woman is preferred.

Although the East End group has had a full complement of officers for the past six years, many A.A. groups cannot and do not maintain such a table of organization. In these cases, usually where the group membership is limited, one or two key people may hold several positions simultaneously. The Lantern group is an example. One member has been chairman and treasurer for two years and a second person has been secretary, program chairman, and intergroup delegate for the same period.

STEERING COMMITTEE

The Steering Committee consists of all current officers and the immediate past chairman. It is the policy making body of the group and decides all procedural matters. For example, in December, 1960, the Steering Committee held a meeting to decide whether or not to give the church in which its meetings are held a Christmas donation. This had been the group policy in past years and it was decided to continue the practice. Small monetary gifts were voted for the caretakers in the church who assist in setting up the room for meetings and who clean up afterward.

The Committee may resolve a variety of situations such as: whether group members should clean up after meetings or help should be hired; how much rent should be paid to the church; how much the group should contribute to General Service and

Intergroup; and whether the group should have a special meeting to commemorate its founding date.

Conferences are not scheduled on a regular basis but are called by the chairman when the need arises. There were six Steering Committee meetings from a December 15th to June 15th period and only two such meetings during the following six months. No specific rules determine the activities of this body and a strong group chairman may make many unilateral decisions without consulting the Committee. On the other hand, any member of the Committee may decide that there is an urgent matter which requires a group decision and a meeting will be called. Even when such meetings are called there is seldom perfect attendance. Two or three members of the Committee are usually absent but decisions are made nevertheless because there are no rules requiring a quorum. These actions may not be announced to the group as a whole but become apparent when they are put into effect.

No minutes are kept and no records maintained. It is apparent that there is almost total dependence on the memory of the older members concerning the precedents for current activities. The most frequently heard comment at such meetings is "This is the way we did it last year," or "This is the reason we do things this way." Tradition and custom are the predominant forces in guiding the activities of the Steering Committee.

GROUP CHAIRMAN

The group chairman is elected for a six-month term and may not succeed himself. He may serve as chairman again after a lapse of two years. There is no job description or any other formal definition of role prescriptions for this office.

The extent of the authority invested in the chairman is largely self-determined, depending upon the personality of the individual filling the post. He (or she) is nominally in charge of group activities and acts as coordinator of all functions. He may make decisions affecting group policy or he may consult with the Steering Committee before taking any important action.

Subordinate officers always confer with the chairman prior to formulating plans and also report to him about activities in their own areas of responsibility. For instance the Intergroup delegate may have attended a special meeting, in which case he will transmit anything of consequence to the chairman. Similarly, the General Service representative will keep the chairman advised about his activities, as will all other officers in their respective functions. Obviously one of the most important duties of the chairman is to coordinate these diverse operations and to insure a free flow of communication.

The chairman also opens all meetings. He calls the meeting to order and then reads the A.A. Preamble to the assemblage. The chairman may then explain the purpose of the meeting. If it is a closed meeting he will tell the gathering that its participation is solicited and that the success of the meeting depends upon contributions to the discussion. He will then introduce the A.A. member who is to act as leader and moderator for that session.

The chairman is expected to arrive at the meeting place at least one half hour before the official starting time. He checks to see that chairs are set up, that coat racks are available, that coffee is being prepared, that cookies, milk, and sugar have been purchased and that generally all preparations for the meeting have been or are being completed. Additionally, the chairman greets group members as they come into the meeting room and welcomes new people with whom he may not be acquainted. The East End group is occasionally visited by out-of-towners. The chairman introduces himself to these visitors and invites them to return to the East End group whenever they are in New York. There are usually one or two people attending their first A.A. meeting and the chairman takes special care to meet such persons and to make certain that a group member looks after these "newcomers."

During the meeting the chairman is responsible for maintaining order. Members will look to him to quiet a person who is disrupting the proceedings. He is also responsible for reminding the leader or speakers that the meeting should not run over the official closing time of 10:00 P.M. The chairman may also have to intercede at closed meetings if he feels that too much time is being taken up with one question thus leaving little opportunity for additional discussion of other problems.

After the meeting the chairman congratulates the speakers and then circulates among the people engaging the visitors and newcomers in conversation. "Sponsors"[1] always introduce new "pigeons"[2] to the chairman.

The East End group boasts that it has never had a chairman who has "slipped"[3] since the group was activated. Obviously there is considerable social pressure on the chairman to be a model of sobriety. Secondly, the choice of chairman always centers on a reliable and substantially sober member of the group. East End has never had a chairman who has been in A.A. for less than one full year.

In addition to his other responsibilities the chairman will also answer questions and offer guidance to any individual member of the group. He will be asked to speak at other A.A. meetings and to lead closed meetings more frequently than other members because of the prominence of his position and the fact that he meets more A.A. people than does the ordinary member.

Finally, the chairman must appoint the nominating committee for the selection of the next slate of officers. He will offer his personal opinion as to those he thinks best suited for various posts. He is in a good position to do this because he has become well acquainted with all the members during his six-month tenure.

In June, 1960, the Steering Committee decided that the position of chairman was so burdensome that he should be allowed to select a member to act as his assistant for the six-month period. The assistant would not be elected but would be appointed by the chairman at his discretion. The chairman in office on June 15th appointed such an assistant, but there was so little actual need for him that the idea was abandoned.

THE SECRETARY

The position of secretary is the second most important in the group. Although East End has no official rules about this, the post is usually filled by a female if the chairman is male and by a male if the chairman is female. In the past two years there have been three females and one male secretary.

The first thing the secretary must do upon assuming office is to send the new list of officers and Twelfth Step contacts to Intergroup where a central listing of all A.A. groups in the metropolitan area is maintained. This is facilitated by completing a form supplied by Intergroup. The secretary also compiles a new and complete list of all current East End members as of the time she takes office. The old membership list is given to her by the past secretary and new names are added. The problem of dropping old members who have not attended meetings for the past six months always arouses controversy.

The secretary takes inventory of all A.A. books and literature in stock and if the supply is low she will send an order to General Service for a bulk quantity which should last at least three months. Most of the literature consists of a large variety of pamphlets for which the group is billed but distributes free. A.A. books are sold by the group at its cost except for the "Big Book" on which a fifty cent sales fee is allowed. The A.A. *Grapevine* is also sold at meetings at a very slight profit. All such sales are handled by the secretary with funds being turned over to the treasurer to help defray the group's expenses.

The secretary receives all communications, bulletins, and notices directly from Intergroup and General Service, as well as various announcements from other A.A. groups. Information of interest is brought to the attention of the chairman and is either read to the group at the meeting or posted on the bulletin board which the secretary keeps up-to-date.

The secretary is also responsible for ordering and purchasing incidental supplies and equipment needed to run the meetings. Paper cups for coffee and cold drinks, napkins, coffee, punch, sugar, milk, cake, and cookies are all purchased or ordered by the secretary. She must also recruit several female members to serve the refreshments at the conclusion of the meeting.

The secretary assists the chairman in greeting members before each meeting gets underway. At the halfway mark the leader of the meeting declares an intermission for the secretary's announcements. During this break the secretary addresses the entire assemblage. First she welcomes all persons present and thanks the speakers for their talks or discussions. She then reads a few short messages, if they are important, and indicates that other announcements of interest are posted on the bulletin board. Attention is called to the free literature which is available and to the variety of A.A. books which are for sale.

After these announcements the secretary recites a line which is part of A.A. ritual at all meetings: "There are no dues or fees in A.A. but we do have expenses and the girls will pass the baskets." Two female members have been asked before the meeting if they will take up the collection, and at this time they pass the baskets around for individual contributions which are turned over to the treasurer the same night.

The secretary is also the group contact for Twelfth Step calls referred by Intergroup. Most such calls are directed to the secretary who may then call on other group members to pursue the matter further. She must also maintain a close liaison with the program chairman because the secretary has to announce the leaders and speakers of future meetings. Her presence is required at least one half hour before the meeting opens, and she is usually the last one to leave because the literature and books have to be put away and all other supplies properly stored.

THE TREASURER

The treasurer is responsible for maintaining records and for banking (or keeping secure) the funds. One of the problems heard at various A.A. meetings concerns the treasurer who gets drunk and uses the group's money for this purpose, or else just disappears from the group, taking the money with him. This is not a frequent occurrence but does happen on rare occasions.

Although the amount of money accumulated at the local group level is seldom very large, some funds are absolutely necessary for group maintenance. Money is needed for rent and for coffee and cookies, the minimal group requirements.

The treasurer at East End opens a checking account in his own name and deposits all money collected. Because his term of office extends for only six months, each new treasurer has to open an original, separate checking account in his own name. Such an account must be kept apart from any other checking or savings accounts which the treasurer may have. Several problems arise from this system. Because of group and individual anonymity, should anything happen to the treasurer the group would not be able to recover the funds. This is an entirely informal procedure in which the treasurer is almost completely on his own. The last four treasurers have submitted periodic reports to the group chairman concerning all monetary matters. One year ago the treasurer instituted a complete bookkeeping system which is now an accurate record of all financial transactions.

The treasurer is responsible for paying all bills. This includes rent to the church, caretakers' services, donations to Intergroup, donations to General Service, charges for literature and books, and bills for paper cups, plates, and napkins. Cookies, coffee, and milk are usually purchased for cash.

The treasurer is in an ambivalent position with regard to the A.A. tradition of respecting and maintaining anonymity. Checks in payment of bills bearing his signature are sent to commercial non-A.A. organizations thus revealing his identity as a member of the organization. This same problem arises when he opens the checking account. A past treasurer reports that when she first went to the bank she was told that if anything happened to her there would be no way for a second party to recover the funds on deposit. She finally told the bank officer that she was a member of A.A., which is a violation of tradition but was necessary on this occasion. The bank officer was quite solicitous and told her that certain safeguards might be taken. However, because the balance never exceeds $200, the group decided that it would not bother with any precautions to guard against such loss. So far East End has never lost any funds because of the death or disappearance of a treasurer. Also, since the inception of the group thirteen years ago, no treasurer has had a "slip" while holding office.

The treasurer submits periodic financial accounts to the chairman and may be called upon to report the status of the group's finances. He presents a formal detailed statement to the group at the last business meeting prior to relinquishing office. When he turns over his records and balance to the new treasurer he also closes his checking account at the bank. The treasurer is usually considered a prime candidate for another office in the group.

THE PROGRAM CHAIRMAN

The program chairman is the "booking agent" of the local group. It is his responsibility to schedule East End speaking engagements at other A.A. groups for their open meetings. He also provides East End "leaders" for closed meetings at different groups. At the same time the program chairman arranges for visiting speakers and leaders for all open and closed meetings of the East End group. These plans are usually completed at an "exchange" meeting arranged by Intergroup every three months, in which program chairmen of most A.A. groups come together for this purpose.

The program chairman has wide discretion as to the scheduling of meetings. The position is usually filled by an older member who has wide personal acquaintance with A.A. people. The East End program chairman at this writing has been in A.A. for eight years and has held several other offices. He is familiar with A.A. personnel and knows the geographic location of most groups. This is rather important because a team of speakers may be reluctant to travel a long distance so that such engagements are limited preferably to the more accessible areas.

The program chairman's knowledge and familiarity with groups is also important with respect to the social hierarchy which exists in A.A. Some groups have more prestige than others and the program chairman will try to "book" either incoming or outgoing meetings with high status groups. This is not always possible; so a wider range is usually necessary. Some groups have the reputation of sending "good" speaking teams while some groups are known as "better" audiences.

The program chairman may complete the schedule for three months or may leave some incoming and outgoing dates open to be filled by group members. He feels a sense of responsibility for the performance of the speakers at incoming meetings and is anxious to have interesting and stimulating sessions.

GENERAL SERVICE REPRESENTATIVE

"A General Service representative is any member of a group elected by that group to act primarily as a connecting link between his group and General Service Headquarters."[4] This is the only position which is formally described in A.A. literature.

The General Service representative is an exception to the tradition that officers serve for only six months in one position. The term for this office is two years. The representative receives all communications from General Service Headquarters and relays these to the local group. Because General Service is supposed to act for and on behalf of the local group it is important that the representative convey the attitudes and wishes of the local group to this headquarters.

General Service Headquarters is maintained largely by voluntary donations from local A.A. groups. The representative is responsible for soliciting these funds from local members every six months or once a year, whichever is more feasible. General Service recommends that donations be based on three dollars per annum per member. The representative solicits this amount and turns the funds over to the treasurer who sends a check to Headquarters.

The representative attends state and provincial assemblies, participating in the election of delegates and committeemen. He is supposed to keep in touch with the delegate from his area who advises him of the local group's opinion on current A.A. matters so that the delegate will be well informed when attending the annual General Service Conference held in New York in April of each year.

The General Service representative may be either male or female. East End has had two consecutive female representatives, each serving the full two years. It is important that this person be a firmly established member of the local group in order to complete the two-year tenure satisfactorily.

THE INTERGROUP DELEGATE

The Intergroup delegate represents the local group at all Intergroup meetings and conferences. He formerly served for six months but in December, 1960, it was decided by the Steering Committee of East End that continuity might better be maintained if this tenure was extended to a full year. The current Intergroup delegate also thought this would be better and agreed to serve a second six months. All future delegates will be elected for one year. The delegate, in this case a male, indicated that it takes three or four months to become familiar with the details of the position so that by the time a six-month term is over he is just becoming effective.

The delegate is authorized to vote for East End at Intergroup when the local group's decisions are solicited. He also recruits volunteers from East End to serve in the Intergroup office as receptionists or to answer telephone inquiries. He reports to the group chairman every week on new developments and also offers a summary of his activities to the entire group at the last business meeting of each six-month period.

THE INSTITUTIONS REPRESENTATIVE

This position was originally intended for six months service but just as in the case of the Intergroup delegate it was extended for an additional period. Future representatives will be elected for a full year.

The chief function of this office is to arrange for East End speaking teams to visit various institutions in the metropolitan area. These include mental institutions, hospitals, Veterans Administration facilities, prisons, Salvation Army centers and similar places where alcoholics may be confined. These engagements are arranged at a meeting of all A.A. Institutions representatives held every three months. Such sessions are attended by representatives of the institutions themselves who request that local groups arrange for speakers to visit them. A regular schedule is then worked out for a full three-month period.

These meetings also offer an opportunity for all local A.A. group Institutions representatives to exchange information and to evaluate the effectiveness of their speaking teams. Many local group members are reluctant to speak at institutions for various reasons and the representative may have some difficulty in filling the schedule. There is a limited response to such requests at East End but the present representative is an aggressive young lady who exerts pressure on the members until they agree. On the other hand some members feel that speaking at institutions is the highest form of work in A.A. and take special pride in volunteering for such engagements.

SUMMARY

An organization chart does not really illustrate all of the facets of the formal structure. Official goals, procedural rules, and institutionalized sanctions are an integral part of the total system. It is clear that the extent and scope of the organizational operations and activities largely determine the elaborateness of the overall organization.

The emergence of these formal patterns in Alcoholics Anonymous is overt evidence of the rapid growth of the organization, particularly with respect to its bureaucratic features. The foregoing discussion has revealed that both the national and local units of A.A. manifest typical characteristics of a formal system in terms of the division of labor, delegation of authority, and channels of communication.

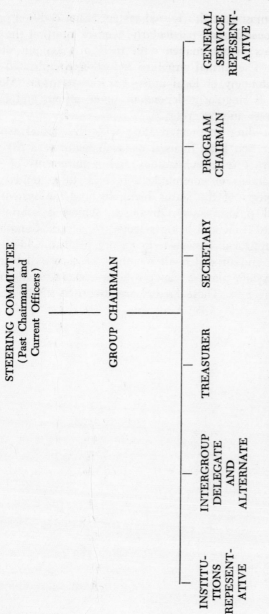

FIGURE 2. Elements in the Formal Structure of the East End Group

For the most part this formal system is not codified or documented. Local groups, particularly, tend to interpret the official requirements in accordance with their own unique situations and needs. The formal structure is further complicated by the relative autonomy of local units. For these reasons Alcoholics Anoymous is singularly dependent upon custom and tradition for perpetuity and progress.

The preceding chapters dealing with the formal aspects of the organization have focused on such features as the organizational structure, specifications and requirements of various offices, channels of communication, and, to a limited extent, certain aspects of the status hierarchy and the system of rewards and punishments. Obviously, achieving sobriety is a reward unto itself and being selected for office is another sign of group approval. However, in an organization which stresses anonymity and in which all members are social deviants, the informal system plays a major role in organizational solidarity and effectiveness. These factors are discussed in the following sections.

CHAPTER FOUR

The Informal Structure of the East End Group

The informal structure of an organization may be viewed as the patterns of behavior that arise out of the spontaneous interaction of individuals and groups and which may not be officially recognized and regulated. The broad framework consists of an internal power structure, techniques for social control, and a system of norms.

A significant characteristic of Alcoholics Anonymous, at the local group level, is the absence of clearly defined and codified rules, regulations, and role prescriptions. Becoming an A.A. participant requires a process of socialization which depends upon custom and tradition transmitted by informal means of communication.

The Twelve Steps and Twelve Traditions offer a limited guide to individual and group performance, but the most pervasive and persuasive force operative in the group is custom. For this reason the informal structure, with its heavy emphasis on interpersonal relationships, is vital to the continued effectiveness and perpetuation of the group.

A prime function of the informal system in A.A. is to insure group continuity. A completely new slate of officers every six months would result in chaos if not for the informal network of authority and communication.

Despite the regular rotation of officers control of the group remains fairly constant and is lodged in the hands of a relatively small power elite. There are three key persons in the East End group, none of whom is currently an officer. They are Mr. R., member of East End for six years; Mr. B., member of East End for nine years; Miss F., member of East End since its inception. Most major decisions are made only after consulting at least one of these members despite the existence of a formal Steering Committee for such purposes.

An example of the influence of these key persons was manifested in November, 1960. The East End group was preparing for its tenth anniversary and the current officers were making no extra preparations for this event. Miss F. approached the chairman and asked him if he intended to have a special meeting on the night of the anniversary. The chairman advised her that as far as he was concerned this would be just another regular meeting, held in the usual fashion. The program chairman was consulted and indicated that she also felt that no extraordinary arrangements were required and that a regular team of speakers from another group had been scheduled. This did not suit Miss F. and she consulted with Mr. R. about the matter. Mr. R. agreed that the anniversary was a special event and that plans should be made to mark that day with a more elaborate ceremony. The chairman and program chairman objected strenuously but they were told that it was the custom of the group to have some kind of celebration to commemorate the founding date.

In the face of such opposition the chairman and program chairman yielded and Mr. R. was appointed to attend to the arrangements for the meeting. He decided that it would be appropriate to have five previous chairmen speak for ten minutes each. The program chairman objected and said that she would like to select the speakers for the meeting because this was essentially her responsibility. Her protest was rejected by Miss F. and Mr. R. and the meeting was finally held according to the dictates of the power coalition.

The selection of officers in December, 1960, was another demonstration of the importance of the key members. The outgoing chairman had personally indicated his choice of a new slate of officers and had made some preliminary investigation to determine whether or not these people would be willing to serve. He was advised by Mr. R. that the correct procedure was to appoint a nominating committee which would make the selection of the new candidates. The chairman said it would be more difficult to find a nominating committee than it would be to select the officers. Nevertheless he was obliged to comply with the policy specified by Mr. R.

The nominating committee met and before any decisions were made, Mr. R. was consulted about the fitness of the nominees. In this respect he virtually exercised veto power over the appointed nominating committee and certainly evinced far more influence than did the chairman. In organizational matters, Mr. R. is the most important individual in the group and exercises the most authority.

It must be remembered, however, that the maintenance of sobriety is still the foremost function of Alcoholics Anonymous and that in this respect Mr. B. is the individual with the most "know-how" and rates highest in the prestige hierarchy. Difficult questions concerning drinking problems are most frequently referred to him. Length of sobriety is an important factor in determining the position of an individual in the status system and Mr. B. has had the longest such period, not having had a drink in over twenty years.

The chairman was approached by a member of the group who said that she knew a married couple who were alcoholics and were currently in serious trouble. The husband was in an alcoholic stupor and the wife had begged this member for help. The member then asked the chairman for guidance. The chairman in turn requested the assistance of Mr. B. who was more adequately able to cope with the situation. Mr. B. is most respected for his pragmatic approach and reliable counsel. He is an excellent Twelfth Stepper and attends every meeting except when out of town or on vacation. For these reasons he is important in the power structure of the informal system.

The participation of individuals in most voluntary organizations is segmental. They do not devote a major share of their time and energy to the association and consider such activity as secondary to their major responsibilities in life. However, the alcoholic in A.A. feels almost completely dependent upon the group for his continued sobriety. This leads to a much greater degree of interpersonal involvement on the informal level. His affiliation with the group is of ultimate importance and is not subordinate to other pursuits.

The formation of primary groups and cliques extends beyond the formal sessions. Meetings are not the principal source of interpersonal contact and communication for many group members. Because the problem of maintaining sobriety is not seasonal, nor temporary, nor confined to the hours of nine to five, alcoholics depend upon social interaction with other group members at all times and especially on Sundays and holidays. One of the most frequently quoted slogans is that "A.A. is a way of life." Many of the members of East End, and of other A.A. groups, form their most intimate friendships among their fellow alcoholics. The following examples illustrate these points.

On a Sunday morning Mr. P. received a telephone call from another member of the East End group. An alcoholic friend of the caller had been arrested the night before and was now in the Municipal Jail at Centre Street in New York City. Mr. P. was asked if he could possibly get down to the courthouse that morning because the case was to be heard by a judge and the alcoholic desperately needed assistance.

Mr. P. said he would go, and despite the protests of his wife, who said that it was Sunday and he should spend the time with his family, drove to the court. Inquiring into the precise whereabouts of the offender, Mr. J., it was learned that the case was to be heard around eleven A.M. Mr. P. identified himself as a member of Alcoholics Anonymous and asked if he could speak with the prisoner or with the judge prior to the hearing. It is important to note that one of the formal prescriptions in A.A. is the preservation of anonymity at all times, but Mr. P. broke this code. The response to his request, as a member of Alcoholics Anonymous, was most favorable indicating the popular and positive image which A.A. has achieved in the public eye.

The prisoner was brought into the court room and Mr. P. was permitted to speak with him for a few minutes. Mr. J. said that he had been drinking heavily the night before and got into a fight. During the dispute he cut his hand and went to a nearby hospital for treatment. While at the hospital he had gone berserk and had smashed some furniture and fought with the doctors. At this point he was arrested by the police and brought to the Centre Street station. Because his family had long since given up on him he had called a friend he had met at an A.A. meeting. He was without funds and had no means to hire a lawyer.

His case was called and the judge said that more time would be needed to obtain the past record; so a new hearing was set for three days later. Mr. P. agreed to return at that time despite the fact that it was a regular work day and he would have to take time off from his job.

On the day of the hearing Mr. P. appeared early and had an opportunity to speak with the judge in his chambers. The jurist indicated that Mr. J. had a number of previous arrests on his record, all as a result of excessive drinking. Mr. P. was commended by the judge for his interest in the case. The judge said he was familiar with the fine work that A.A. was doing. At no time was Mr. P. asked for identification or some proof of membership. Actually there is no formal identification or membership card available in A.A. Many members carry an A.A. meeting list which apparently satisfies the need when it arises.

The judge said that he would like to send Mr. J. to Bellevue for observation after which a final determination would be made. Mr. J. was called into the chambers and was asked if he had anything to say for himself before action was taken. Having no real defense Mr. J. said that he was not responsible for his behavior because he was an alcoholic and suffering from a compulsion which he could not control. This infuriated the judge who said that the defendant was simply trying to exploit the situation.

A ten day stay for observation in Bellevue was ordered at which time the case would be resolved. Mr. P. gave Mr. J. a few dollars to purchase some personal items and said that he would be back in ten days. During this period Mr. P. went to Bellevue twice to see if he could be of any further assistance. At the time of final action Mr. P. appeared with the defendant while the judge passed sentence. Mr. J. was put on probation and was told that one condition was regular attendance at A.A. meetings. Mr. P. assured the court that he would personally see to it that this was properly executed. That same night Mr. P. went to an A.A. meeting with Mr. J. and continued this practice for the next twenty-one nights, not missing a single meeting. Mr. J. was quite nervous for the first few days and he needed, and received, a great deal of attention from Mr. P., including a small loan to hold him until he found a job. Mr. P. invited him to dinner every night for the first week and then twice a week afterwards.

After four weeks Mr. P. reduced his own attendance at meetings but made certain that Mr. J. continued to participate in the A.A. program. This very close association has continued until the present and Mr. J. has now been "dry"[1] for eleven months. He has a job and his entire outlook on life has improved.

The preceding case demonstrates the extent of time and energy involved in total participation in the program. It also illustrates some of the informal patterns which arise in coping with immediate problems without specifically defined rules and prescriptions. No two people do Twelfth Step work in the same fashion. It is a matter of playing it "by ear" with a few basic directions from old-timers supplementing one's own experience.

Another case illustrates a member's reluctance to become too deeply involved with an alcoholic in need of help.

Richard, an alcoholic who had finally reached his "bottom"[2] called Intergroup asking to be put into a hospital. Intergroup contacted the East End group secretary who, in turn, called a member, Mr. D. Because, by tradition, two people are supposed to go out on Twelfth Step calls, Mr. D. telephoned an A.A. associate and together they went to Richard's home. Richard was indeed in poor condition, lying in bed with four or five empty vodka bottles on the floor. However, after waiting for about two hours the A.A.'s were able to explain the purpose of their visit to Richard. In accordance with customary procedures, Mr. D. and his friend described their own drinking experiences and how A.A. had helped them to recovery.

By this time Richard was able to walk with support and they proceeded to Town's Hospital in New York City. Richard was admitted and assigned to a room. The "cure" lasts five days and largely consists of drying out and some A.A. therapy. The fee must be paid in advance and alcoholics will not be admitted a second time within six months. This is to cut down on the "revolving door" of alcoholics drying out, getting drunk and then drying out again in the hospital. There are no other hospitals in New York City which admit alcoholics; so some veteran drinkers have devised some ingenious schemes for getting into the psychiatric wards of Bellevue or Kings County.

Mr. D. signed Richard into the hospital thus assuming the role of "sponsor." Either he or another A.A. member must appear on the fifth day to sign the patient out. It is also expected that the "sponsor" will visit his "pigeon" at least once, and more often if possible, during the five days.

Mr. D. signed Richard out on the fifth day, which happened to be Saturday. He was aware that he should take Richard to an A.A. meeting that night but he had a social engagement himself. He had tried to locate another member who might take over for him on this night but could not do so. After leaving the hospital Mr. D. advised Richard to go home and rest and that he would call him the following morning. On Sunday Mr. D. called Richard and suggested that they go to a meeting together that night. This was arranged and after the meeting Mr. D. recommended that they continue this practice for at least a week. Richard was living with his wife in a small apartment and Mr. D. was invited to dinner a few nights later. The wife was most appreciative and expressed deep gratitude for what Mr. D. was doing.

This close relationship continued for another ten days at which time Mr. D. had a discussion with Richard and informed him that he thought it might be appropriate if Richard became a little more independent and did not rely on anyone to such a great extent. Richard was reassured that Mr. D. would always be available when and if needed and that they certainly would see each other at meetings. They did meet at the East End group twice a week but no strong bond was formed although Richard did call Mr. D. at home a few times. In about three months Richard stopped coming to meetings and Mr. D. called him to find out just what might be wrong. He was advised that Richard was feeling much better and did not think he needed to attend any more sessions.

About four months later a member of East End told Mr. D. that she had met Richard and that he had been drinking again. Mr. D. called him at home but Richard said that he had the situation under control and that he had returned to drinking "socially." Two months later Richard's wife called to say that he was quite sick and could Mr. D. please come over. Mr. D. did this and Richard and he went to an A.A. meeting as soon as Richard was able to do so. Mr. D. was still reluctant to form a more durable relationship with Richard who evidently was unable to manage by himself. At the present writing Mr. D. has not seen Richard for three months.

The preceding cases serve to illustrate the lack of a clearly defined or firmly established method for dealing with some highly important phases of A.A. activity. The only standard operating procedure is informal and evolves out of the experience of the members. Each member must meet the exigencies of the moment on an individual basis, relying upon the advice and support he himself has received from other members, added to his own personal experiences. The "right" way and the "wrong" way of coping with certain situations are learned in the socialization process and comprise much of the discussion at closed meetings.

Other manifestations of informal structure emerge at open meetings. These sessions consist of visiting teams of speakers from other groups who rotate or exchange meetings periodically. At each meeting a leader and two or three other speakers relate their drinking and recovery experiences. These speakers are supposed to represent one particular A.A. group. Nevertheless, about one third of the time all the speakers do not actually belong to the group designated that night. This fact is usually not announced to the audience, although occasionally a speaker will say, "Although I am talking on behalf of the Random group, I am really a member of the Boulevard group. However, Danny called me earlier this evening and asked me if I could fill in for one of his people who couldn't make it. I'm glad to be here."

Many groups have a limited number of members, not all of whom are willing or able to fill speaking obligations. Because the group wants to participate in the total A.A. program it books outgoing meetings at other groups. It frequently happens that two or three members are not available on the night they are supposed to speak so the leader may call some friends at other groups to substitute. This is a reciprocal arrangement and members of East End have often been called upon to help some other group in need of speakers. If the formal group lines were rigidly maintained the program of open meetings would be seriously impaired.

Although East End has a program chairman who is supposed to arrange all incoming and outgoing meetings, "private" bookings usually circumvent this formal procedure. East End members may speak as a team at some other group without going through channels when the request comes directly to one or another of the members who enlists his own participants for this engagement.

Although the open meetings are part of A.A. therapy, they are often judged by the members of the audience on the basis of interest or entertainment value. After each open meeting the host group, in this case East End, congratulates the speakers for presenting a "wonderful" meeting. Privately many of the members evaluate the meeting and offer some critical appraisal of the speakers. Meetings thus can be very interesting, exciting, dull, funny, strange, or mediocre. The speakers too are discussed on the basis of their performances—some are called sincere, some too dramatic, some dull, and some very touching and warm.

Much of the same kind of evaluation is made of closed meetings and the leaders of these sessions. Although the procedure for conducting such meetings is fairly uniform, the leader himself may be forceful or shy, may dominate the discussion or may allow the group to participate to a great extent, and may actually limit such dialogue; in other words the format may be fixed but the tone and style of the meeting are established by the leader.

Another aspect of the informal organization is the development of an argot unique to Alcoholics Anonymous.[3] Much of this special language emerges from the activities, rituals and artifacts intrinsic to the A.A. program. Certain elements of the argot have been adopted from the jargon of the more general drinking culture. Although most members of Alcoholics Anonymous are familiar with the universal language of drinkers, the converse is not true. A term such as "civilians" refers to those people on the outside of A.A., including heavy drinkers, social imbibers, and teetotalers.

The A.A. argot serves to make the association more cohesive. It sharpens the delineation between in-groups and out-groups and strengthens the feeling of belonging and sharing in something special. Other people may go on a rescue mission, perform errands of mercy, participate in social welfare activities, but only a member of A.A. goes on a Twelfth Step call. An alcoholic can feel that he is part of the fellowship when he is not only a member of A.A. but is identified as *an* A.A.

The rituals also serve to re-enforce group solidarity. Rites of passage and rites of intensification are part of the informal system. The specific names of these ceremonials are also incorporated in the argot of the organization.

When a newcomer speaks at an open meeting for the first time this fact is made known to the audience who congratulates him at the conclusion of his talk. Most of the alcoholics present make a special point of commending him for his initial effort. Some members of A.A. are reluctant to speak at open meetings and postpone their first talks far beyond the three-month probationary period. For the neophyte his speaking debut is a special event and is marked as such by the members of A.A.

"Anniversaries" and "birthdays" are also celebrated in the various local groups. When a member attains one year of

sobriety his first "birthday" is recognized and occasionally pub-
licized within A.A. His group may send an announcement to
all secretaries in the metropolitan area asking them to announce
the fact that the East End group is having a special meeting
to celebrate the "birthday" or "anniversary" of Mr. K. A special
cake is usually purchased on this occasion and the close friends
of the celebrant present him with some gifts. The speakers for
such meetings are usually his "sponsor" and other people closely
associated with his entry into A.A.

Bill W.'s "anniversary" is the annual occasion for a ceremonial
dinner at a leading New York hotel. This year the price of a
ticket to the dinner was $9.00. Any excess proceeds are donated
to Intergroup which arranges the affair.

Cliques, or friendship groups, are also prevalent in A.A. This
is partly due to the nature of induction of new members in
the "sponsor"-"pigeon" relationship. A new member frequently
affiliates with the associates of his "sponsor." Most cliques are
formed on the basis of common interests and age compatability.
Strong clique formations sometimes emerge among the old-
timers who tend to be the elders of the group and represent
an informal vested interest coterie.

Cliques may consist of a number of members who came into
the program at approximately the same time, somewhat like
a college freshman class. Such people might find much in
common because they are undergoing the same experiences and
passing through the same stages of socialization.

Cliques in A.A. are sometimes antagonistic and occasionally
are expressions of rivalries. The key figures in the power elite
may not belong to the same friendship group. Generally, however, such coteries in the East End group serve as a therapeutic
force, expedite communications, and contribute to ultimate
group solidarity. They extend the A.A. program beyond the
physical boundaries of meeting halls.

Patterns of Group Membership

DEFINITION OF MEMBERSHIP

As indicated in the A.A. Preamble. "The only requirement for membership is a desire to stop drinking." This is taken literally. There are no further limitations or restrictions on joining the program or affiliating with a group. There are no dues nor fees, no pledges, no oaths, and no minimum number of meetings to be attended. No formal membership lists are maintained nor does an individual have to enroll officially. Membership is self-defined and self-maintained. No person in A.A. has the authority, right, or privilege to deny affiliation to any individual who has a desire to stop drinking.

The question of membership determination is so vague that statistics quoted about the number of participants in A.A. must be carefully appraised. At the present time A.A. claims a total of 300,000 members but this is largely an unverified tabulation. This was recognized by the General Service Board when it undertook a complete census in the latter part of 1960. A letter from General Service was sent to all local group secretaries with an enclosed census card and group information form. The special A.A. census card called for the name of the group, number of *active members,* and number of *non-participating members.* The grand total is assumed to be the actual membership of the group. However, there are no criteria by which to classify non-participating members. Presumably these would be alcoholics who do not attend meetings and do not take part in group activities. It would seem impossible to verify that such people are actually affiliated with a group; in fact, they may no longer be sober and may have dropped out of A.A. Added to this is the fact that many groups do not maintain membership lists or if they do they are of questionable reliability.

On January 1, 1960, official East End membership comprised forty-eight names. Six months later the list was revised and reduced to forty-two, a loss of eight members. This roster is still the subject of controversy in the group. Contributions to Intergroup and General Service are based on a count of thirty members which indicates that even the list of forty-two names is not precise and is so recognized by the leaders of East End. Some of the older members insist that the roster should be revised and that people who do not attend meetings or take part in group activities be dropped. Because there are no objective criteria for determining group membership this is difficult to accomplish.

Table 1 shows the attendance record of the members of East End for a six-month period, including open and closed meetings. Indicative of the vague interpretation of the membership classification is the fact that seven persons did not attend a single meeting during this period and five others appeared less than six times out of a possible total of fifty-three sessions.

When the roster was reviewed by the Steering Committee it was suggested that flagrant absentees be dropped from the group. However, in every case it was reported that the individuals concerned were all active in the program and continued to identify themselves as members of East End. These people had maintained a minimal degree of informal contact with East Enders who were able to confirm their sobriety and group affiliation despite their poor attendance records.

It is also true that a certain number of alcoholics do not like to attend meetings but carry out other A.A. responsibilities effectively. There are also those who prefer open meetings and never appear at closed sessions. Still others seldom miss a closed discussion but are rarely in evidence at open meetings. It is apparent that attendance at meetings is not an absolute criterion for determining group membership. The critical factors appear to be self-identification and a minimal degree of informal contact.

TABLE 1.—Total Meetings Attended June 15-December 15, 1960

Member	Open Meetings	Closed Meetings
A	0	0
B	0	0
C	0	0
D	0	0
E	0	0
F	19	0
G	25	24
H	10	8
I	8	11
J	2	0
K	9	14
L	23	23
M	10	10
N	3	3
0	19	16
P	18	18
Q	22	21
R	20	20
S	0	26
T	1	2
U	10	0
V	19	14
W	21	18
X	7	9
Y	23	20
Z	16	15
BB	1	22
CC	3	5
DD	4	6
EE	21	18
FF	0	0
GG	0	1
HH	2	3
II	1	2
JJ	5	21
KK	0	0
LL	17	16
MM	10	26
NN	20	21
OO	19	2
PP	3	0
QQ	16	12

Maximum number of open meetings this period — 27
Maximum number of closed meetings this period — 26

RECRUITING MEMBERS

There are a number of ways by which a group may add to its membership:

1. Referred to East End by Intergroup.
2. Friend or relative of an East End member with no prior A.A. contact.
3. Twelfth Step call by East End member.
4. Transfer from another local group to East End.
5. Transfer from out-of-town group by alcoholic who has moved to New York.
6. Members of East End who have dropped out of A.A. and who have now returned.

THE NEW MEMBER

The new member may come into A.A. on his own or under the protective guidance of a "sponsor." If he decides to select a "sponsor," or if by circumstance he already has one, his indoctrination and socialization into A.A. will be expedited. There are several ways by which a new member may acquire a "sponsor."

1. Before entering A.A. he may call Intergroup and ask for help. If he is not incapacitated he will be directed to the nearest A.A. meeting in his area that night. However, if he has any serious physical or emotional difficulty it may be suggested that he voluntarily enter Town's Hospital in New York City for the five-day treatment. If he does not actually require hospitalization but feels that he needs more help than merely being directed to an A.A. meeting, two members of an A.A. group in his vicinity will visit him.

These A.A.'s will call upon him at his residence and offer him whatever aid, assistance, and advice they can. They will personally escort him to a meeting that night and will continue to do so for an indeterminate period. The newcomer may establish close rapport with one of these A.A.'s who will then become his "sponsor" and will be largely responsible for guiding the "pigeon" through his early weeks in the program. The "sponsor" must be prepared to spend considerable time and effort in helping his "pigeon." The degree of such involvement depends upon the specific situation, but there is a definite obligation towards the "pigeon" on the part of the "sponsor."

2. As previously discussed, a newcomer may acquire a "sponsor" in the process of being hospitalized.

3. The third way a novice may obtain a "sponsor" is by voluntary selection. The neophyte who joins a group without any previous associations may feel that he would prefer the guidance of an older member. He then requests an individual to be his "sponsor" and if the member agrees, as he should, the relationship may continue indefinitely.

A person may join an A.A. group without benefit of a "sponsor" and without ever adopting one. He may participate in group activities and attend meetings by himself, forming friendships as he goes along. Forty per cent of East End members never had a "sponsor" nor did they express the need for one. Some members reveal a strong distaste for the entire relationship and indicate a preference for friends in A.A., but not "sponsors." This may be illustrated by a conversation with a female member of East End, age thirty-five, sober eighteen months.

I heard about A.A. from a friend of mine and went to my first meeting by myself. This was a rough time for me but I looked around and thought that these people had been helped so maybe I might find some way out of the mess as well. I continued to come to meetings of East End but was very shy and spoke to nobody at first. After a few weeks some members began to have conversations with me and I started having coffee with some of them after meetings. It was suggested that maybe I ought to ask somebody to be my "sponsor" but I didn't like the idea of being supervised or dominated by the person. I told them that I preferred getting to know people just as I had been doing by attending meetings and participating in A.A. activity.

Over a period of time I did become close friends with Eve. She and I just hit it off together. I never considered her my "sponsor" and she never thought of me as a "pigeon" but we became good friends and still are today. Naturally

I talk to her about my problems more than with other A.A. members but I also get considerable help and advice from several other people. I find this relationship much better for me; it leaves me free to go to whichever meetings I wish and I feel no obligation to a "sponsor." Besides sometimes it's hard to get rid of a "sponsor" after you feel you would like to do so.

I do not like to be a "sponsor." Certainly I have helped some people get into A.A. and have continued to associate with them—not as a "sponsor," but as a friend.

DECREASE IN GROUP MEMBERSHIP

A group may suffer loss of membership in the following ways:

1. Members who drop out of A.A.
2. Members who transfer to other groups in New York City.
3. Members who move out-of-town.
4. Members whose "sponsors" transfer to other groups and who prefer to move with them.
5. Members who "slip" and who are ashamed to return to their original group but affiliate with a different A.A. unit.

THE FEMALE MEMBER

For the female, being an alcoholic is far more debilitating than it is for the male counterpart. Despite the trend toward greater permissiveness and participation in drinking behavior by the contemporary female, such activity is still regarded largely as being within the male domain. This is especially so with reference to heavy drinking. Intoxication, no matter what the degree, is a privilege reserved exclusively for the American male. The female inebriate is the object of social censure and is looked upon with disdain and contempt for violating her sex role prescriptions. A drunken woman is certainly a more tragic figure than her male equivalent.

The female problem drinker finds her behavior totally incompatible with her normative social roles. Whether she be a wife, mother, or career girl, she still occupies the primary status of female with its concomitant social responsibilities. The continuing emancipation of the American female and the blurring of the distinction between the sex roles in recent times has allowed women a greater degree of freedom to participate in the approved patterns of drinking behavior in the total culture. However, female inebriation and excessive drinking is still widely condemned, and violators of the norms in this area may expect severe sanctions.

The extent of female alcoholism is simply not known. It is difficult enough, if not impossible, to determine with any degree of precision the number of alcoholics in this country. All available statistics are only estimates, are subject to critical appraisal, and should be treated with reservation and qualification. The question of the proportion of alcoholics who are females is further complicated by the nature of their drinking habits in which subterfuge and deceit play a more prominent part. Most females who drink excessively do so in the privacy of their homes or apartments because the mores still prohibit such activity in public places. The woman, therefore, even more so than the man, is prone to be the hidden alcoholic. However, the impact on her life and on those associated with her, be they husband, children, parents, or friends, is devastating.

No attempt is made here to characterize the female alcoholic as some homogeneous type. There is probably no accurate composite picture of the female problem drinker any more than there is for the male inebriate. Yet this need not deter us from recognizing the unique issues involved in understanding and coping with female alcoholism. In this respect Alcoholics Anonymous offers a physical and psychological haven for the troubled woman drinker.

Just as with the overall membership, there are no precise figures concerning the number of women in A.A. In the East End group they comprise forty per cent of the total. The range in A.A. extends from no females to as high as fifty per cent in some groups. To an extent this is determined by geographic location of the group, social class milieu, and the presence of other women in the group. There are no official restrictions on female affiliation, although some groups are known to be predominantly male. Despite the paucity of data there appears to be a larger proportion of females in A.A. than would be expected from their ratio in the alcoholic population.

For the woman problem drinker A.A. may prove to be especially gratifying. She has met with defeat in life and her chronic drinking has usually resulted in her being rejected and her feelings of inadequacy being re-enforced. Invariably she has been ostracized by her peers. This behavioral syndrome is particularly traumatic for a woman and affects all areas of her life, including interaction with the significant persons with whom she may be associated. A husband may express shock or disgust at his alcoholic wife; a child will experience shame and fear for his alcoholic mother; the parental family will manifest tremendous anxiety. If she is single or divorced she will find it impossible to establish satisfactory relationships with a male while she is an active alcoholic. In business or the professional world she is similarly deprived of security and stability. This entire negative perspective, a consequence of her uncontrolled drinking, may be reversed in A.A.

In the fellowship she is received with approbation, warmth, and acceptance. She notices other females who have also suffered as she has and who apparently have been able to rebuild their lives. Her status as a female is enhanced and supported. She is not the object of degradation or exploitation and begins to interact with male members with more ease and assurance. There have even been a number of A.A. marriages, although romantic activities are not actually encouraged. Nevertheless one should not discount the importance of being an accepted part of a heterosexual society. As we shall see later in this volume, the female A.A. is highly regarded and pursues many activities in the organization.

The special problems of the female alcoholic and the process of affiliation with A.A. may best be illustrated by two case histories. These are the stories of two female alcoholics as related at open meetings at A.A. Although they are individual cases they do present the general picture of the difficulties encountered by the female alcoholic.

CASE 1. *Eva G. Age forty.*

Eva is an alcoholic who had her first drink at the age of twenty when she was in college. Her parents did not drink too much although there was always liquor in the house for guests. She never had any particular desire to drink and even when she went out on dates she would order ginger ale or coke. In college, however, she decided that one or two drinks would not hurt, particularly at parties where everybody seemed to be drinking anyhow.

Eva then became a social drinker and did not have any problems with liquor. After she graduated she got a job in the advertising department of a large department store and married one of the executives about two years later. She still did not experience any difficulty with alcohol although she did drink on weekends. Eva had two children, both boys, and moved to the suburbs where she and her husband purchased a house. She noticed that her drinking was increasing to the point where she was having a cocktail before dinner every night in addition to some weekend and party drinking.

The first time she got really drunk was at a New Year's party where she passed out and her husband had to take her home. She was thoroughly ashamed and promised herself that she would not repeat the performance. Her husband also began to express some concern about her drinking but she assured him that she could handle things and there was no need for alarm. Eva did control her drinking for the next few months but found a need for a late afternoon pick-up too much to resist. By this time both children were attending school and Eva had more free time on her hands.

Eva became more and more involved with her drinking and purchased a bottle of scotch which she kept hidden from her husband. Her husband noticed alcohol on her breath almost every day when he came home from work. He became worried about the children, and arguments became routine. Eva denied that she was drinking too much (a very common trait of people having drinking problems) and claimed that her husband was exaggerating.

Meanwhile Eva was beginning to consume two bottles of whiskey a week by herself and financial problems started to be a factor. On more than one occasion the children returned from school to find their mother asleep on the couch and had some difficulty in arousing her.

Eva's husband finally suggested that she visit a psychiatrist because their family life was being destroyed by her drinking. The people in the community were worried when Eva became drunk at dinners or parties to which she was invited. Eva finally decided to discuss the problem with her priest and hoped that she would be able to stop drinking as a result.

Things did not get better and Eva's drinking was reaching a point of desperation. In addition she began to use sleeping pills and soon found it impossible to get through a night without them. Finally Eva could hardly wait for the children to leave the house in the morning so that she could have a few drinks to steady her nerves. Her husband threatened to leave her several times and finally told her that for the sake of the children he would have to have the marriage ended unless she went to a psychiatrist. Eva finally consented but did not take her psychiatric sessions seriously and frequently was half drunk when she went for her therapy. The drinking continued unabated.

Eva's mental and physical condition deteriorated to such an extent that she was ultimately hospitalized and spent three months in a private rest home. She swore when she was discharged that she would never touch a drop of liquor again. Within three months Eva was drunk again and this time her husband asked that divorce proceedings be undertaken. The divorce was granted and her husband took custody of the children.

Eva returned to work and lived in an apartment by herself in New York City. The job lasted only four months until she was discharged for being absent too often. This was quite true because Eva usually did not report for work on Mondays after a weekend of drinking.

Two other jobs were lost in similar fashion and Eva's spirits were at the lowest point of her existence. As she said, and as many other alcoholics have reiterated, "I was sick and tired of being sick and tired." On her last job, just before she was fired, one of the girls with whom she became friendly suggested that Eva was drinking too much and that she ought to cut down. This girl's sister was an alcoholic and had joined A.A. and she wondered whether Eva had ever considered such a move. Eva denied that she had a drinking problem and advised the girl that she was perfectly able to handle her own affairs.

Nevertheless during one desperate drinking bout one weekend Eva called the girl and asked her if she could contact her sister. The sister called and arranged to come over to Eva's apartment. The place was a mess because Eva's major concern over the past months was solely with drinking, not with housekeeping. She was thoroughly ashamed but nevertheless permitted the sister to enter the apartment with another woman from A.A. The two ladies discussed their own drinking problems and explained how they had been helped by A.A. It was suggested that the three of them go to a meeting at the East End group that night. Eva had become a virtual recluse and her venture out that night was her first social experience in quite some time. She was filled with fear and apprehension but went to her first A.A. meeting.

She was impressed by the presence of quite a number of well-dressed women who admitted that they were alcoholics and could not handle alcohol. Eva was struck by the lack of shame and guilt when these women discussed their problems with alcohol and she determined that she too would stop drinking. However, it was not quite that simple. The sister became Eva's "sponsor" and they went to three or four meetings a week but it was not until four months later that Eva finally had her last drink. She has been sober now for fourteen months and feels a great deal of pride in this achievement. Her sense of dignity and self-respect is being restored and slowly she is finding her way back into the mainstream of society.

CASE 2. *Marjorie P. Age fifty-five.*

Marjorie comes from a family in which heavy drinking was quite common. Her father was an alcoholic and one of her brothers also had difficulty with liquor. She remembers most about her childhood the constant abuse which her mother received because her father had been drinking. Marjorie grew up with an abiding hatred of her father which did not diminish until she joined A.A. and learned that alcoholism is a sickness, a disease which must be understood not condemned.

Marjorie vowed that she would never drink because of what she saw happening in her own family. However, this was not to be. Marjorie had her first drink at a party when she was seventeen and liked the effect immediately. It made her forget her troubles for awhile and she found that she was no longer shy and timid after a few drinks. She graduated from high school and found a job as a stenographer. Conditions at home became so bad that Marjorie was compelled to move out. She went to the Y.W.C.A. and lived there for about a year until she was able to rent an apartment which she shared with a girl from her office.

Marjorie attended the usual number of parties during the next few years and went out on dates three or four times a month. She found that she could not really enjoy herself unless she had a few drinks during the course of the evening. It was difficult for her to have as many drinks as she would like on a date because her escort would not think it right. She took to carrying a small bottle in her purse and would go to the ladies room to fortify herself if she found the need too strong.

When Marjorie was thirty-two she met a man with whom she fell in love and he asked her to marry him. She tried to conceal her drinking habits from him but on almost every occasion, be it dinner or going to a dance, Marjorie would become inebriated. The man withdrew his marriage offer and Marjorie's drinking went from bad to worse.

She eventually lost her job with the company where she had been employed for fifteen years. Her father died in the interim and she had to send some money to her mother who was quite ill. The girl with whom she shared the apartment could not tolerate Marjorie's excessive drinking and moved out leaving Marjorie completely alone.

She was able to reduce her drinking somewhat and found another job. She moved from the apartment into a furnished room where she isolated herself and spent most weekends in a state of intoxication. Her drinking during the week was more controlled but she soon found that the evenings were too long without a few drinks to kill the time.

After one particularly bad weekend she blacked out and the landlady of the rooming house had to call an ambulance. Marjorie was hospitalized for ten days and was then able to return to work. Her drinking continued and her life became unmanageable. On one occasion she attempted suicide and was sent to Bellevue for observation. While in the hospital it was suggested that she try A.A. and she agreed to do so.

She called A.A. and was sent to the East End group which had a meeting that night. She walked into the meeting room but was overcome with anxiety and did not stay. However, she returned for the next meeting and was greeted by a female member. After this initial contact Marjorie was successful in limiting her drinking and after her third meeting she was able to stop drinking entirely. She never married and feels that most of her life was ruined by alcohol. However, she is determined to make the best of her situation and feels secure in A.A. She has been "dry" for seven years.

CHAPTER SIX

Group Activities

The primary purpose of the A.A. program is to enable the members to maintain sobriety and to help others achieve this objective. There are various activities which are directly and indirectly involved in accomplishing this goal. Speakers at meetings often refer to A.A. as a "selfish program," meaning that all activity in which the individual takes part ultimately helps his own sobriety. A popular A.A. slogan states that "you have to give it away to keep it."

ATTENDANCE AT MEETINGS

The foremost activity prescribed for members is attending meetings. Although this is considered essential for continued sobriety few members appear at every group session. The question of the number of meetings an alcoholic should attend is discussed frequently at closed meetings but no minimum is specifically advised because the need differs for each person.

Newcomers are urged to go to a meeting every night until they achieve a modicum of security. Old-timers also insist that neglecting these sessions leads to trouble. The A.A. meeting is considered an essential part of recovery and is compared to the insulin which keeps diabetics alive.

Although it is said that whenever two alcoholics come together there is an A.A. meeting, satisfaction is expressed by members when there is a "full house." Since closed meetings are primarily for the purpose of discussion, a group of twenty-five is considered to be the maximum suitable for this purpose. Attendance at some East End closed meetings has gone as high as fifty-two, which makes the procedure somewhat cumbersome. The largest open meeting at East End occurred the night of an anniversary meeting at which time one hundred and nineteen people were present. The usual attendance at open meetings is sixty-five to seventy.

Many A.A.'s are acquainted with other members of various groups. Because no single group has more than two meetings per week (one open and one closed), affiliates of a local group will visit other units on nights when their own meetings are not scheduled. There is a definite preference among A.A.'s for certain groups, based upon evaluation passed along by word of mouth. With respect to social class composition, A.A. groups are quite homogeneous within themselves although there is a wide range across the total organization. Members exercise a process of self-selection by which they fit themselves into a group at their own social class level. This finding is supported by Lofland and Lejeune.[1] Newcomers are also received differentially depending upon overt manifestations of social class.[2]

If a regular member misses meetings for two or three consecutive weeks, and if no contact has been made with other A.A.'s, somebody will call to investigate the reason for the prolonged absence. There is a certain amount of security in belonging to a group because members are concerned about each other's welfare. Some A.A.'s do not affiliate with any single group but go to meetings wherever and whenever they please. There is no rule which stipulates that an alcoholic must belong to a particular group.

Social pressure is exerted on members to attend meetings. During the bitter snowstorm of December 12, 1960, and the following frigid days, attendance at most A.A. groups was below normal. Those members who did attend remarked in sardonic fashion that a little cold, snow, or ice never kept alcoholics away from a saloon but now that they were feeling better they did not think meetings were too important.

Meetings are held by other voluntary associations for various purposes but seldom do such meetings focus directly on the therapeutic process. Many voluntary associations are dedicated to helping others. Alcoholics Anonymous is a self-help program. What is done is done for one's own sake and for one's own sobriety. Speakers at open meetings invariably comment, "If nobody here has been helped tonight, we certainly have helped ourselves."

TYPES OF A.A. MEETINGS

There are several formats for meetings in A.A.:

1. The Open Meeting
2. The Closed Meeting
3. The Beginners Meeting
4. The Institution Meeting

The Open Meeting: This meeting is open to alcoholics and the general public. For the most part it is attended by members of the local group, their relatives and friends, newcomers referred by Intergroup, a few members of other A.A. groups, and some "civilians"[3] interested in the general problem of alcoholism.

A team consisting of a leader and two or three speakers who represent some other A.A. group is introduced by the local group chairman. Usually at least one female will be included in the team so that women in the audience will feel a stronger identification. The leader of the team tells an abbreviated version of his "story," taking perhaps ten minutes, and then introduces his first speaker. The speaker will recount his drinking experiences and recovery in A.A., taking about fifteen minutes to do so. At the conclusion of his talk the audience responds with applause and the leader then introduces the next speaker. At the termination of the second presentation the leader calls for the local group's secretary to make her announcements.

The group secretary thanks the speakers for their talks and then reads any special notices to the audience. These may include the anniversary meetings of other groups or any other important A.A. activity. She will also announce the speakers for the following week's meetings. An invitation is then extended to all to stay for refreshments after the meeting. A request is made to all newcomers to introduce themselves to other members and to leave their names with the secretary if they so desire. The secretary announces that "A.A. has no dues or fees, but we do have expenses, and the girls will pass the baskets." At this point two ladies pass around the collection baskets for donations from the assemblage.

At the conclusion of this ritual the leader resumes the regular meeting and introduces the last speaker. All meetings are scheduled to end at ten o'clock. "No souls saved after ten" is a commonly used slogan. Only on rare occasions will the speakers go beyond this deadline.

When the last speaker concludes his story the leader sums up and usually states that this was "a typical A.A. meeting, but if you did not get anything out of this meeting, just keep coming." All meetings are terminated with the recitation of the Lord's Prayer. The chairs are put away and the audience moves to the area where coffee and cookies are being served.

This is the "coffee therapy" during which time informal discussions are held between small groups, and newcomers have an opportunity to meet some of the older members. The conversations are almost exclusively devoted to the topic of alcoholism and the advantages derived from participation in the A.A. program. This coffee period usually lasts for thirty to forty-five minutes. Two or three groups of members may then go to a nearby coffee shop for further conversations which may last for another hour or two.

The Closed Meeting: The second major type of meeting is the closed or discussion session for alcoholics only.

On one occasion an alcoholic visitor from out-of-town attended a closed meeting with her husband. It was not until the meeting was over that it was discovered that her husband was not an alcoholic and was only keeping his wife company. When this fact was called to the attention of the members, the alcoholic wife and the husband were advised that closed meetings were not intended for entertainment purposes and his attendance was considered a breach of A.A. principles. However, and this is somewhat paradoxical, it is assumed that all persons attending such meetings are actually alcoholics, by self-definition, and nobody has the right to challenge the presence of any individual.

The closed meeting itself is an authentic form of group psychotherapy and is referred to by many members as the "workshop" of A.A. The format varies slightly in different areas but the basic idea is the same. Each week the meeting is conducted by a member of a different local group so that one person will seldom lead the same closed meeting more than once in several years. At the East End group written questions are submitted to the discussion leader before the meeting starts. Some groups use verbal questions from the floor but essentially the technique is identical.

The leader "qualifies"[4] by reciting a short history of his drinking experience and his recovery in A.A. This usually takes five or ten minutes. After this brief story the leader will read the first question and then offer his personal suggestions as to the best way to cope with the problem presented. Suggestions are then solicited from other group members. There are no restrictions on individual participation. Anybody can offer comments, advice, or even criticism of previous recommendations. Discussion is seldom cut off until everybody desiring to do so has had an opportunity to speak. Some questions may take just one or two minutes to answer, or in some cases the discussion may be carried on for half an hour.

An average of eight problems are discussed at each session. During the course of this research three hundred questions submitted for discussion were obtained. A sample of these items follows:

Do you have to join a group right away, or can you wait and select one after a little while?

In your case history (just related) what would you say was the one alcoholic incident which would best serve to qualify you as an alcoholic?

I find it unrewarding and uncomfortable to 12 Step people with a drinking problem in early stages or at a very young age. Very few in my experience continue to come around after a few months. I don't feel alcoholism can be prevented and dislike the feeling of proselytizing.

I heard a speaker say one night that if you are truly grateful you do not have self-pity, resentments, and the desire to drink. Comments?

Do you think alcoholism is a personality disease?

I am sober in A.A. a short time and attending meetings regularly but now have reason to review the first step. Please discuss.

If holidays have always made it tough for you in the past how do you make it doubly safe on a day like tomorrow (Christmas)?

They tell me that I should just try to stay sober a day at a time but that I can never safely take another drink. How come?

Please discuss making amends, its objectives and its limitations.

If you have been dry awhile and get upset when someone insists you take a drink, do you think this is bad?

How do you reach the ability to pick up the phone before you pick up the glass?

Will you please elaborate on the A.A. saying "First Things First." Thank you.

I have heard that people who really eat well and regularly, and have always done so, can stand daily copious quantities of alcohol with relative impunity. What do you think?

I gather one is supposed to "surrender" before one really "gets" the A.A. program. If this is so, how can one do this and possibly function well enough to get on in this demanding and competitive society? Maybe I misunderstood "surrender."

Please discuss the 2nd Step.

What are some of the ways to apply the program to "all our affairs?"

What about a chap who has been coming to A.A. for five years and still says he does not think he is an alcoholic? Do you just forget him? Or do you help him to understand? He says he takes a drink now and then.

Discuss happy sobriety.

Do you think that the illness called alcoholism progresses automatically during the span of sobriety of the former drinker?

Why, when I have been sober for three months will I still have to go to meetings?

At the mid-point of the meeting the leader calls a halt to the proceedings and the secretary makes her announcements. At this time the collection is taken up. The secretary also thanks the leader for the way in which he is conducting the session. After this brief intermission the discussion is resumed until approximately 10:00 P.M., at which time the leader brings the meeting to a close. Written questions which have not been answered are turned over to the secretary to be held for the following week. The leader usually thanks the group for its participation and requests all who wish to, to join in the Lord's Prayer.

After this ritual the chairs are put aside and coffee and cookies are served. The "coffee therapy" continues for about half an hour after which several members may gather for some additional conversation at a nearby coffee shop or restaurant.

The Beginners Meeting: This is another type of closed meeting which is held by some local groups during the hour preceding a regular session. This meeting is conducted by a reliable member of the group with a fairly long period of sobriety and, as the name implies, is intended for newcomers to A.A.

Although this is also a discussion meeting the orientation is toward helping a newcomer get acquainted with A.A. techniques, norms, and procedures. The first few days and weeks in A.A. are most difficult for some people and these beginners meetings are structured to help them through this trying period.

The Institution Meeting: This may be either a closed or an open meeting depending upon the type of institution involved. Here the major concern is with the patients at a hospital, or the inmates in a jail, or the down-and-outer at a Salvation Army center. Some group members are reluctant to speak at institutions, particularly mental hospitals, because they find the atmosphere depressing. Others take special pride in being able to help such people. The type of response which speakers find at these institutions also varies. In many cases the inmates attend such meetings for purposes other than an interest in achieving sobriety. For instance it may look good on the record of an inmate if he attends A.A. meetings, or it may relieve the monotony of hospital routine. Usually this is an opportunity to stay up later and have special refreshments. Nevertheless, it is hoped that people in institutions will continue to attend A.A. meetings after their period of confinement.

SPEAKING AT OPEN MEETINGS

After a member achieves three months' sobriety he is permitted to represent the East End group as part of a speaking team. He will, if he so desires, participate in outgoing meetings just as other A.A. groups send speaking teams to East End for its open sessions. Some members do not prefer to speak at open meetings, feeling completely inhibited by having to address an audience ranging in size from fifteen to one hundred. Even accomplished public speakers in A.A. express a degree of anxiety just before they get up to tell their stories.

LEADING A CLOSED MEETING

This activity is also available to members who have achieved a minimum of three months' sobriety. Those alcoholics who are too timid or shy and refuse to speak at open meetings are equally reluctant to lead a discussion where they are completely on their own. Implicit in this function is a degree of sophistication and knowledge concerning the mechanics of Alcoholics Anonymous. Additionally the leader has to be able to control the group so that a meaningful discussion is generated and maintained.

Usually a closed meeting is conducted away from the home group, which means that for the most part the leader is in strange surroundings facing unfamiliar people. This adds to the stage fright of the alcoholic. However, those who do lead closed meetings express considerable satisfaction and indicate that they have benefited to a great extent by such participation.

An important factor to note is that the leaders and discussants in these group sessions are not professionals but are alcoholics who have had no training in therapeutic techniques. The insights expressed at these meetings and the soundness of the advice proferred evolve from practical experience. While the leader is the moving force, the opinions of other members are solicited so that each participant derives some benefit from the sessions. On the average only twenty-five per cent of those attending closed meetings actually offer suggestions or make comments, the rest just listen, identify with the discussants, and, hopefully, absorb helpful information.

TWELFTH STEP WORK

The Twelfth Step reads, "Having had a spiritual awakening as the result of these steps we tried to carry this message to alcoholics, and to practice these principles in all our affairs."[5] Twelfth Step work refers to answering calls for help from alcoholics in distress. The norms strongly re-enforce this activity, and seldom does an A.A. refuse to honor a request for assistance.

There are no rules or regulations concerning the proper technique for executing a Twelfth Step call nor are the responsibilities of the member defined for such situations. Because this activity is so essential to individual and group survival, and because basic rules are not spelled out, there is considerable discussion on this topic at closed meetings and during informal conversations.

Several recommendations are offered by old-timers and others with experience in making such calls.

1. Males should not Twelfth Step females, nor should females go out on Twelfth Step calls for males. This aids the active alcoholic in identifying with a member of his own sex and also acts as a safeguard against any possible sexual involvement.

2. The person in distress must actually ask for assistance and must express a desire to be helped.

3. If possible never go on Twelfth Step calls alone. Two A.A.'s always go together because you never know what difficulties might be encountered.

4. If the person needs medical attention a doctor should be called. Twelfth Step work does not mean involvement in administering medical treatment.

5. If the person needs hospitalization, suitable arrangements should be made through Intergroup to have him admitted to Town's Hospital.

6. A.A. assistance means showing a person the way to sobriety, offering comfort and sympathetic understanding. The Twelfth Stepper ordinarily should not offer financial assistance.

7. If the person is too drunk to understand what is going on, wait until he is more sober, or come back later.

8. Do not give the individual more liquor to drink unless it is to prevent him from going into the D.T.'s.

9. If the person resists or refuses to cooperate, leave.

10. Make suggestions and recommendations in keeping with A.A. tradition.

11. If the person is able, get him to an A.A. meeting as soon as possible. Do not let him procrastinate.

12. Follow up and make sure that he continues to go to A.A. meetings. If the relationship is satisfactory you may become his "sponsor."

13. When first making the Twelfth Step call, the best thing

to do is to tell of your own drinking experiences and recovery in A.A.

14. At least one of the A.A.'s on a call should be experienced in Twelfth Step work.

This guide is not formally prescribed anywhere in the literature but stems from the combined experience of the alcoholics in the program. Members work Twelfth Step calls according to their individual techniques and depending upon the situation.

These calls are not made by professional people. There is no therapeutic training involved nor are there any special devices used. What is effective, apparently, is the principle of one alcoholic talking to another—one recovered, the other seeking help. Such a procedure is contrary to orthodox psychotherapy in which the patient does the talking. No attempt is made to explore motivation or underlying causes.

Twelfth Step work entails considerable involvement by the member and for this reason some are reluctant to participate in this activity. A few cases illustrate the type of situations which may be encountered on Twelfth Step calls.

CASE 1

A call was received at home by Mr. Y., member of the East End group, one evening, around 7:00 P.M. The call was from the wife of an alcoholic who had been drinking for six consecutive days and was now virtually unconscious. The wife called Mr. Y., a friend of hers, because she knew he was in A.A. and thought he might help. Her husband had been drinking heavily for ten years and this was the third or fourth time that he had gone on a binge for a full week. She was afraid that he would lose his job and that their children would suffer unduly.

Mr. Y. knew the family and felt that this was a situation in which he might be of assistance. He called Mr. E., also of the East End group, and asked him if he could help out on a Twelfth Step call. Mr. E. agreed and the two met before proceeding to the home of the alcoholic, Mr. B. When they arrived the wife was frantic and Mr. B. was sprawled out on his bed, dead to the world, with several empty whiskey bottles in the waste paper basket.

The two A.A.'s were unable to awaken Mr. B. His wife advised them that he had not eaten all week and that she was afraid he would go into convulsions, which he had done once before. Mr. Y. called a local physician recommended by Intergroup. The doctor arrived in about half an hour and examined the patient who was now beginning to show some feeble signs of life. He was given a shot of vitamin B_1 and B_{12} which was all the doctor could possibly do.

The two A.A.'s waited another hour at which time Mr. B. became fairly coherent. They asked him if he wanted to sober up and if so they would take him to Town's Hospital where he would have to stay for five days. He agreed and the A.A.'s drove him to the hospital where Mr. Y. signed him into the A.A. ward with the assurance that he would be back to visit Mr. B. within the next few days.

Mr. Y. did visit Mr. B. three days later and on the fifth day he returned to the hospital and signed the patient out. They returned to the home of Mr. B. that afternoon and the same night went to an East End closed meeting. For the next twenty-one days they went to a meeting together every night. In addition, Mr. B. would call Mr. Y. on the telephone occasionally because he felt depressed or because he had an urge to take a drink. Gradually Mr. B.'s condition improved to the point where he went to meetings by himself and reached a period of three months without a drink. At this point Mr. Y. would meet Mr. B. at the East End meetings and they would have coffee together and talk matters over.

Things went along this way for two months and then Mr. B. did not show up for two consecutive East End meetings. Mr. Y. called his home and was advised by the wife that her husband was drinking again. She asked Mr. Y. to come over if he could before it was too late. Mr. Y. did get over to the house the next day and met Mr. B. who admitted in a most embarrassed fashion that he had had "just a few beers" but felt very guilty and would like to get back into A.A. Attendance at meetings was resumed.

CASE 2

A call came to the East End secretary from Intergroup indicating that a female alcoholic had asked for help. The secretary called Miss E., a member of East End, asking if she could handle a Twelfth Step call in midtown New York. Miss E. said she would take care of it. This was on a Sunday afternoon and Miss E. could not locate another female A.A. to accompany her; so she called a male member of East End, Mr. S., who went along with her.

They arrived at the apartment in a midtown hotel and were received by a thin, elderly lady of about sixty. She was in tears and kept repeating that she wanted to stop drinking but just could not and felt like killing herself. Because this was a female, Mr. S. let Miss E. take the initiative. Miss E. told the lady that they were from A.A. and that they fully understood the problem. The lady refused to believe that Miss E. had ever been an alcoholic so Miss E. related some of her drinking experiences and how she had been helped by Alcoholics Anonymous. This did not accomplish very much because the lady kept crying and now started to say that God had let her down although she prayed and prayed but to no avail.

Mr. S. and Miss E. spent the next two hours talking to the lady, who was somewhat calmer by now. She was asked if she would like to go to an A.A. meeting the next day and she readily agreed. Miss E. then told her that the best time to stop drinking was right now and they might as well get rid of any liquor that was in the apartment. The lady assured them that there was nothing but a few empty bottles in the garbage and that was all.

Miss E. looked under the bed and found three full fifths of whiskey and suggested that they might as well spill these down the toilet. The lady became furious and told them to "get the hell out" that she was not going to spill good whiskey down the toilet.

Miss E. asked her if she really did want to stop drinking, and the lady started to cry again, swearing that she did want to but could not. She refused, in no uncertain terms, to surrender the bottles despite the fact that Miss E. said there was nothing that could be done with her if she kept the whiskey. The lady refused to cooperate; so Miss E. left her phone number and told the lady to call if she needed help in the future. The call was never received.

CASE 3

About eight months ago a member of East End group moved to Long Island and no further word was received from him until three months ago when he called the chairman of East End, asking for help because he had been drinking for two weeks and felt that he was going to die unless he was hospitalized. The chairman called two East End members, who drove to the house of Mr. C., about forty miles out on Long Island.

When they arrived he recognized them, although he was quite drunk, and thanked them for coming. His wife was also most grateful and they planned to drive Mr. C. to Town's Hospital in New York City where he would sober up and dry out for five days. Mr. C. insisted that he needed a few more drinks to steady his nerves and the A.A.'s gave him two short drinks. Almost immediately Mr. C. became violent and said he would not go to Town's Hospital and that the A.A.'s were nothing but "phonies" who were trying to put him away in an institution. He became abusive and insisted on finishing the bottle of vodka. When this was done he collapsed on the bed and became violently ill. The A.A.'s thought it best to call a doctor but they could not get one to come; so an ambulance was summoned instead. The hospital refused to admit Mr. C. because he was suffering from alcoholism. The A.A.'s prevailed upon the admitting doctor to put Mr. C. in the psychiatric ward if this was the only alternative. This was accomplished.

The next day one of the A.A.'s drove out to the hospital and did so every other day for ten days until Mr. C. was discharged. Mr. C. is now back in A.A. and has not had a drink since that episode. He admits that he had stopped going to meetings and had no longer participated in A.A. activities prior to his resuming drinking.

These cases serve to indicate the extent of involvement which Twelfth Step work may entail. Even in the simple cases in which the person seeking help cooperates fully and takes to A.A. immediately, the "sponsor" must keep a watchful eye on his "pigeon." Some members of East End do not prolong the period of sponsorship. As soon as the person is sober and going to meetings regularly they advise him that from now on the rest is up to him. He is told that if he wants to stay sober all he has to do is stay close to A.A., if he doesn't he will probably end up drinking again.

Almost every Twelfth Step call is a unique story in itself. No two cases are exactly alike but they do have the common denominator that, regardless of the reason, alcohol is the immediate problem. A popular A.A. slogan posted at all meetings reads, "First Things First." In Twelfth Step calls the first thing is to get the person sober and into the program.

A list of Twelfth Step volunteers for each group is maintained at Intergroup and these members may be called at any time. Because most members work during the day there is a shortage of Twelfth Step volunteers from the hours of nine to five. The list at Intergroup may indicate the office telephone number of the A.A. member as well as the home phone number. East End no longer submits office phone numbers because some calls were being made to members at their places of employment. Such a practice can prove to be harmful, particularly if the employer does not know that the employee being called is in A.A. Paradoxically, citizens receive the plaudits of the community for participating in various voluntary associations but despite the fact that the organization of A.A. is recognized as having accomplished a great deal in treating alcoholism, the individual member may still be stigmatized if it is revealed that he is an alcoholic.

SERVICE AT INTERGROUP

The telephones and service desks at Intergroup are staffed by A.A. volunteers, and every two months East End is asked to send some members, particularly for Sundays or evening hours. This is a good opportunity for members who are reluctant to speak, and who are not good at Twelfth Step work, to make a valuable contribution.

Such service means answering the telephones at Intergroup and making the proper referrals of those calls from people asking for help. Each desk is equipped with a loose leaf book listing every group in the metropolitan area, with the telephone numbers of officers and members available for Twelfth Step work. The first call is usually made to the group secretary and if there is no answer then other members may be tried.

In addition to the telephone calls personal discussions are held with people who come to the Intergroup office seeking help, either for themselves or for their friends or relatives. The A.A. member need not wait until his group is asked to serve but may volunteer for such service whenever he so desires. Some A.A. members have spare time during the day and drop in at Intergroup to see if they can be of help.

GROUP K. P.

Another activity, which may appear to be rather mundane, is nevertheless quite important, especially to newcomers. This consists of a number of chores in the meeting place:

1. Set out chairs in orderly arrangement.
2. Put out ashtrays—one to every two seats.
3. Make coffee (enough for the anticipated crowd).
4. Set out cake or cookies to be served with coffee at conclusion of meeting.
5. Put out A.A. literature and hang A.A. slogans.
6. At the end of the meeting clean up, put away ashtrays, literature, and slogans, and stack chairs neatly.
7. Wash out coffee urns, sweep up, and put trash outside.

Although these tasks appear to be quite menial, to a newcomer they indicate a degree of acceptance. For a person who has experienced nothing but rejection and abuse for long periods of time this can be important. It gives him the feeling that he is making a contribution to the group and that he is actually aiding his own sobriety. Many of these people reached a point in their drinking careers when they gladly performed the lowest type of work just for a few drinks. Now they may be doing some ordinary chores but as part of a program of recovery.

All group members share in performing these tasks, usually with goodwill but occasionally with some grumbling—the same kind of complaining one finds in all social clubs and associations.

CHAPTER SEVEN

The Deviant Deviants

The unconventional character of Alcoholics Anonymous provides us with a rare opportunity to examine the nature of deviancy and social control in an organization composed exclusively of social deviants. Studies of deviant groups are, in themselves, not new to sociology but, as we shall see, A.A. is unique in its definition of deviancy and in its subsequent imposition of sanctions. Since A.A. is probably the only group of deviants condoned by the larger society within which it operates, it has developed into a large-scale voluntary association with an important role in American society.

We concur with Cohen in defining deviancy as "behavior which violates institutionalized expectations, that is, expectations which are shared and recognized as legitimate within a social system."[1]

Commenting upon the development of such expectations Thrasher had this to say:

This unity of the gang rests upon a certain consensus or community of habits, sentiments, and attitudes, which enable the gang members to feel as one, to subordinate themselves and their personal wishes to gang purposes, and to accept the common objectives, beliefs and symbols of the gang as their own.[2]

Thrasher's conclusions are equally applicable to A.A.:

The gang as an intimate primary group, develops an excellent basis for control through rapport. Life together over a more or less extended period results in a common social heritage shared by every member of the group. Common experience of an intimate and often an intense nature prepares the way for close sympathy—for mutual interpretation of subtle signs indicating changes in sentiment or attitude. Collective representations embodied in the signs, symbols (such as the badge in a fraternity), secret grips and words, and the argot of the group, all promote mutual responsiveness in the more subtle forms of communication.[3]

In a similar vein, speaking of street corner society Whyte commented:

The stable composition of the group and the lack of social assurance on the part of its members contribute toward producing a very high rate of social interaction within the group. . . . Out of such interaction there arises a system of mutual obligations which is fundamental to group cohesion.[4]

These institutional expectations are in essence a system of norms. Dubin notes, "We can define institutional norms as the boundaries between prescribed behaviors and proscribed behaviors in a particular institutional setting."[5]

In order for a discussion of deviance to be meaningful it is imperative that the system of regulatory norms be stipulated. A prominent theory maintains that the deviant is in fact participating in a subculture in which his behavior is normative. It is Cohen's major thesis that delinquent boys are participating in social interaction among like-minded deviants who mutually reinforce their deviant attitudes and behavior.[6]

In his analysis of the marihuana user, Becker lends support to the notion that deviant behavior has its origins in a subculture.

. . . breakdowns in social control are often the consequences of the person becoming a participant in a subculture whose controls operate at cross-purposes to those of the larger society.[7]

He continues:

Distribution [of marihuana] is confined to illicit sources which are not available to the ordinary person. In order for a person to begin marihuana use, he must begin participation in some group through which these sources of supply become available to him, ordinarily a group organized around values and activities opposing those of the larger society.[8]

In his classic statement developing a typology of deviant behavior Merton comments, "Socially deviant behavior is just as much a product of social structure as conformist behavior."[9] His central theme is that "deviant behavior may be regarded sociologically as a symptom of dissociation between culturally prescribed aspirations and socially structured avenues for realizing these aspirations."[10] Expanding on this, Cloward remarks:

> Apart from both socially patterned pressures, which give rise to deviance, and from values, which determine choices of adaptations, a further variable should be taken into account: namely, differentials in availability of illegitimate means.[11]

In his critique of Merton's typology, Dubin declares:

> Both of us employ units in the construction of the typologies the definitions of which rest on common understanding among social scientists. Merton analyzes the person's actions with relation to cultural goals and institutionally prescribed means. I add groups to the category of actors.[12]

As an example of group deviant behavior Dubin discusses social movements.

> As a form of group deviant behavior, social movements are characterized by an active search for new cultural goals and modification of existing institutional means. Social movements, however, remain attached to the existing social system through acceptance by their participants of institutional norms in the area of their interests—they are not wholly alienated from the society in which they appear.[13]

In addressing himself to the question of group deviancy Parsons comments:

> The legitimation of a deviant pattern immediately shifts it from the status of an individual to that of a collective phenomenon. Those whose orientations reciprocally legitimate

each other constitute a collectivity which is a sub-system of the social system. It is obvious that when an individual has attained this type of interactive support it becomes immensely more difficult to undermine his motivation to deviance. Very simply his deviance is strongly rewarded.[14]

He indicates that there are two additional factors which strengthen deviant motivations of the collectivity.

The first of these is the degree of difficulty of stigmatizing the sub-culture pattern as illegitimate in terms of the wider value system. . . . The second set of factors which further the claim to legitimation is that involved in the development of a strong defensive morale of the deviant group.[15]

The preceding writers have all been concerned with the development of deviant behavior. The focus of their attention has been the deviant individual or a collectivity of deviant individuals acting within a group structure. In the latter sense, the group as a unit is also conceived of as being deviant.

In this decisive respect Alcoholics Anonymous represents a singular type of system. Although every member is a social deviant the organization itself is not. On the contrary the association is highly regarded by the larger society within which it functions. Additionally, A.A. is not in opposition to the values and goals of the general social order. Its primary function is to return its members to full and active participation in the ongoing society.

However, for the A.A. member there are a number of mitigating factors attached to the resumption of his customary adult role in society. If he is to abide by A.A. norms then in a very real sense he will continue to be a social deviant as a necessary part of his recovery and rehabilitation. In essence this is the paradox of the A.A. program. In several critical respects the A.A.'s course of life differs from that of the ordinary citizen.

1. His status remains permanently that of an "alcoholic."
2. His disease (alcoholism) is arrested, not cured, so that the "therapy" must continue indefinitely.

3. His "therapy" consists of constant and enduring participation in the A.A. program.

4. Above all he must never take the first drink.

Within the bounds of the A.A. organization these prescriptions are not deviant, but rather form the basis of normative expectations and are fundamental to the maintenance of the system. This would indicate that Alcoholics Anonymous is guided by a pattern of indigenous norms. In this respect A.A. diverges from customary organizational development. A fundamental trait of large-scale organizations is that the behavior of the membership is governed by a set of rules, rather than by traditions.[16] Yet, for the most part A.A. people are guided by custom and tradition, not by a set of formal regulations.

This is not to imply that bureaucracy has not developed in A.A., because it has. However, it is the representative type described by Gouldner.

> The representative bureaucracy is, in part, characterized by authority based upon knowledge and expertise. It also entails collaborative or bilateral initiation of the organizational rules by the parties involved; the rules are justified by the participants on the ground that they are means to desired ends, and persuasion and education are used to obtain compliance with them.[17]

Sills, in his analysis of the National Foundation for Infantile Paralysis, reports:

> . . . rules are of course necessary for the efficient day to day conduct of an organization. If every question had to be decided on its own merits, . . . an organization would be able to devote little attention to the conduct of its program.[18]

Rules do exist in A.A. but they are difficult to express in explicit terms. The members of the group can distinguish between what is right and what is wrong but these judgments are not based on a body of laws or regulations. A statement heard frequently in A.A. is, "There are no musts in A.A." The program is referred to as an individual pursuit which each person interprets in accordance with his own needs and desires. Even the basic Twelve Steps for recovery are "suggested," not mandatory.

However, as indicated previously, there is an established normative order with a concomitant system of social control which includes a distinctive definition of deviancy. The nature of deviancy is inextricably interwoven with the unique characteristics of Alcoholics Anonymous.

The purpose of the foregoing discussion was to illustrate some of the theoretical approaches to the study of individual and group deviancy. The major preoccupation of the writers in this field has been with the origins and development of deviancy in our society. Dentler and Erickson summarize the present situation:

> The most widely cited social theories of deviant behavior which have appeared in recent years . . . have helped turn sociologists' attention from earlier models of social pathology in which deviance was seen as direct evidence of disorganization. These newer models have attended to the problem of how social structures exert pressure on certain individuals rather than others toward the expression of deviance. Yet the break with the older social disorganization tradition is only partial, since these theories still regard deviance from the point of view of its value as a "symptom" of dysfunctional structures.[19]

They offer the following interpretations of deviant behavior in enduring primary and task groups:

1. Deviant behavior tends to be induced, permitted, and sustained by a given group.
2. Deviant behavior functions to help maintain group equilibrium.
3. Groups will resist any trend toward alienation of a member whose behavior is deviant.[20]

Although they do not explicitly include "normative" subcultural deviancy in their discussion, Dentler and Erickson note that deviancy must be considered in the context of the social unit in which it prevails. A fundamental precept of this book is that deviant behavior cannot be defined only as an aspect of the personality of the actor but must be evaluated in terms of interaction within a group structure. Whether or not an act is defined as deviant is determined by the system of norms as well as the group's interpretation of the actor's violation of these prescriptions. As we shall see, this is particularly true of Alcoholics Anonymous.

LaPiere's comments about status groups are germane to this theme.

> From the point of view of the individual member, a status group supplies satisfactions that he cannot otherwise secure, provided that he does what is required of him by the group as a whole; i.e., the group grants him rights and exacts in return fulfillment of role obligations. Each member of a status group may more or less clearly perceive his own position in these terms. At the same time, however, he tends to view the position of each of the other members in terms of their adherence to the norms—i.e., the standards of conduct that are held to be right and proper for members of the group. The latter point of view stems from the former; for the status of the individual depends upon the maintenance of the group itself, and the group can exist only if and as long as the members conform more or less exactly to the norms. Aside from whatever distinctive physical similarities they may happen to possess, . . . what makes the members a group is their adherence to standards of conduct which at once distinguish them from non-members and identify them, in their own eyes and in the eyes of non-members, as participants in a common activity.[21]

Group norms constitute the standards which actually guide the behavior of the members. Generally speaking, these "rules" are implied rather than overtly defined. The norms of Alcoholics Anonymous have evolved out of the historical origins of the association and have been reinforced by the continuous and growing interaction of its members. Individual and group experience have been the chief factors in molding the system of mutual expectations. Although the members of Alcoholics Anonymous do not ordinarily think of their norms as comprising a set of rigid demands, they recognize that the road to recovery and the maintenance of sobriety depend upon at least minimal participation in the program.

The nearest thing to a formal set of rules and regulations consists of the Twelve Steps of A.A. for individual recovery and the Twelve Traditions of A.A. for group guidance.[22] These provide the crude framework within which an individual's behavior may be judged as being deviant or proper. In addition, the A.A. preamble offers a succinct account of the association's principles.

Another guidepost for individual recovery consists of a variety of slogans which are conspicuously displayed in most meeting places. There is no uniformity with regard to the way these slogans appear but generally, in one form or another, the following are usually exhibited:

FIRST THINGS FIRST

EASY DOES IT

KEEP IT SIMPLE

LET GO AND LET GOD

IT CAN BE DONE

THINK

LIVE AND LET LIVE

ONE DAY AT A TIME

Finally, the Serenity Prayer is recommended as an invaluable aid in keeping sober. The prayer is printed on wallet-sized cards and is carried on the person of many members. It acts as a sort of "charm": if a person feels an impulse to have a drink he may find strength to resist by reading this invocation. In addition, members feel that the Serenity Prayer provides them with an excellent philosophy for coping with the tensions and stresses of daily life.

Although the slogans and the Serenity Prayer are not, strictly speaking, norm prescriptions they are recommended as tools which the alcoholic should use in his battle with the bottle. When a member has a "slip"—the most striking act of deviancy—others in the group may say that he did not pay attention to one or another of the slogans and therefore was more vulnerable to the compulsion to drink.

Nowhere in the preceding account of A.A. "rules" is there a stipulation that a person must be an alcoholic to qualify as a member. The specific requirement is "a desire to stop drinking." Some years ago the wording was "an *honest* desire to stop drinking" but after considerable discussion the term "honest" was deleted. In essence this means that the individual himself is the only one who can determine whether or not he is an alcoholic regardless of any other objective criteria. It also signifies that the range of difficulty with drinking may extend from the "high bottom"[23] drinker to the "low bottom"[24] drinker. The "desire to stop drinking" hits people at completely different stages of their drinking careers.

A case history may serve to illustrate norm infractions which result from the ambiguity in defining an "alcoholic":

Raymond, age forty-five, member of the East End group, had been a heavy drinker for the past twenty years. About three years ago the situation became acute and he was drunk almost continuously. Because he lived alone and was a bachelor he was able to provide for his needs with part-time jobs. However, his drinking became so bad in the past year that he finally called A.A. for help. He was referred to the East End group where he attended his first meeting. At that time he met Pete and told him that he was not sure if he was an alcoholic but he would like to attend A.A. meetings anyhow.

Pete advised him that there was no hurry and that he ought to keep coming to meetings until he decided whether or not he needed help and wanted to stop drinking. Raymond did just that. He kept coming to meetings, but more often than not he was drunk at these times. After a few weeks he called Pete on a Monday night and said that he was awfully sick and would like to go to the hospital. Arrangements were made by Pete to get Raymond admitted to Town's Hospital for the five-day treatment. During the five days of hospitalization in the A.A. ward Raymond came into close contact with other alcoholics and also attended A.A. meetings every night.

When Pete came around at the end of the five days to sign him out Raymond was in good physical condition. He and Pete attended an A.A. meeting the same night that he was discharged from the hospital. After that Raymond, always in the company of Pete, visited a different A.A. group nightly until he had achieved a degree of stability. He still would not admit that he was an alcoholic and Pete never insisted, merely indicating that he had to make up his own mind about that.

After Raymond had been dry for almost three months he had a discussion with Pete during which he expressed his appreciation for all that A.A. had done for him. He was sober, had found a new job, felt fine and all of his friends had commented on his robust appearance. Everybody was delighted with his progress—especially Pete. Raymond still maintained that he was not sure he was an alcoholic. Now that he was feeling better he was inclined to think that his problems with liquor were over and that he could drink socially. This whole idea is a severe violation of A.A. principles and Pete cautioned him that if he started to drink he would end up in the hospital again in short order.

A few weeks later Raymond came to an East End meeting and told Pete that he had had a few cocktails before dinner and that he felt fine. This is a serious norm violation and the most severe form of deviancy in A.A. but Raymond was not sharply reprimanded. In fact just the opposite occurred. Because of his deviant act the members felt that he needed A.A. more than ever so that instead of rejecting Raymond he was the focus of some extra attention on the part of the members in their attempt to explain the nature of alcoholism to him. Even when he denied that he was an alcoholic he was not excluded from the group but was told to keep coming to meetings.

Strangely, despite his denial of alcoholism, Raymond maintained his attendance. Now, however, he was noticeably drunk at a number of sessions and finally this resulted in another breach of the norms, not by Raymond, but by an East End member.

At the end of one meeting Raymond spilled a cup of coffee on a member's suit. The member, Phil, told Raymond that he ought to be more careful. A brief argument followed and Phil finally told Raymond that he did not see why he (Raymond) came to meetings at all if he was so sure that he was not an alcoholic. Raymond agreed that he was not an alcoholic at which point Phil told him that he ought to get out and stay out, that A.A. was only for alcoholics. Raymond left in a hurry and never returned to the East End group.

Phil felt guilty and apologized to Pete saying that he had no right to take anybody's inventory and that Raymond had as much right to be in A.A. as anybody else. He added that nobody had the right to judge anybody else and certainly nobody was justified or authorized to tell another person to leave the group. Although the members tried to rationalize Phil's behavior he felt conscience stricken and called Raymond the next day to express his regrets.

This incident supports Dentler and Erickson's proposition that in some cases "groups will resist any trend toward alienation of a member whose behavior is deviant."[25] Raymond's behavior was certainly deviant in several ways. He refused to admit that he was an alcoholic and resisted the idea that he was different from other heavy social drinkers; this, despite all evidence to the contrary. He continued, while drunk to attend meetings, behavior which is hardly encouraged in A.A. Nevertheless the normative group reaction to such behavior is tolerance and sympathy. In this respect Phil's behavior and not Raymond's was defined as deviant because Phil did not adhere to the group's expectations of dealing with such a situation. One of the strongest norms in A.A., although not codified, is the prohibition against "taking somebody else's inventory." In other words you are not to pass judgment on the behavior of another member. Phil violated this norm when he challenged Raymond's right to participate in A.A. It was not within his domain to determine whether or not Raymond "had a desire to stop drinking."

Furthermore, Phil disregarded the Twelfth Step—"Having had a spiritual awakening as the result of these steps, we tried to carry this message to alcoholics, and to practice these principles in all our affairs." This is the basis for the strong emphasis on helping other drunks, something Phil forgot. If Phil felt that Raymond was having trouble he should have been especially solicitous.

At the present writing a somewhat similar case is being conducted in strict accordance with A.A. norms.

Roslyn is married, age about thirty-five, attractive and has had a problem with her drinking for the past eight or ten years. Her husband has abandoned all hope and has indicated that he would like nothing better than a divorce. Roslyn first contacted A.A. eighteen months ago, and attended meetings regularly for the first three months, during which time she did not have a drink. She then had a "slip" but kept coming to meetings. Soon her "slips" became more frequent and she started coming to meetings with liquor on her breath. However, her "sponsor" was not discouraged and despite the fact that Roslyn did not seem able to stay away from her first drink no resentment was shown. The "sponsor" patiently continued her relationship with Roslyn despite an apparent lack of success. The longest period of sobriety that Roslyn has been able to sustain is two months but the "sponsor" is hopeful at this time that long-term sobriety may be achieved ultimately.

Another example illustrates the way in which the group reacts to and interprets deviancy.

Joe came to the East End group three years ago and had difficulty in getting sober. It was not until he had been in A.A. for six months that he was finally able to put a number of "twenty-four hours" of sobriety together in succession. He did make it, though, and soon was able to boast of one full year's sobriety.

Because of his new found stability and the fact that he

was active in group affairs, Joe was elected to the position of group secretary for the usual term of six months. He talked of how wonderful his life had become since he was able to stay sober. Among his new accomplishments was a good job and a fairly nice apartment in New York. His wife, who had been on the verge of divorce, had returned and they were together for the first time in five years.

After being in office for two months Joe did not appear for three consecutive meetings. Two of the East End members called his residence but got no answer. The next week two members visited Joe's apartment and found his wife home alone. She informed them that Joe had started drinking three weeks ago and she had not seen him for five days. The members told her that if she should hear from Joe to tell him that they were worried about him and that he should call one of them or just come back to the group.

During meetings whenever Joe's name was brought up in a discussion he was never the object of negative remarks. Without fail the members expressed interest and concern. "I sure hope he has enough sense to come back when he gets off this one" was a typical comment. Joe did return after three more weeks elapsed and the members were delighted to see him. One of the members who had closely associated with Joe said that he would sure keep his eye out so that this did not happen again.

Joe's story is representative of all A.A.'s who "slip." Negative sanctions are not imposed and the group responds with considerable empathy. There are a small number of alcoholics who have been affiliated with A.A. for as long as ten years but who have not been able to stay sober for any length of time. Nevertheless they continue to attend meetings and when they are able to do so they participate in other activities of the program.

In this respect the deviant actor is the A.A. who is not tolerant or sympathetic, even though he himself has been sober for years without a "slip." Chastisement of those who "slip" is frowned upon.

The case of the A.A. who has a "slip" is clearly defined as aberrant behavior. There is not always similar consensus about other situations in A.A., so that it is sometimes difficult to determine whether an act is deviant in any given context. The following case illustrates this point.

Byron was a new member of East End, having been in for six months, during which time he was completely sober. Like all people new to any organization he had been learning the "rules of the game." A number of times Byron had been approached by a "down-and-out" alcoholic and had been asked for a handout. Not knowing what the "rules" were Byron usually gave these fellows fifty cents.

One night, Dan, an old-timer in A.A., saw Byron give one of these "bums" some money and told him that this practice was frowned upon in East End, and, in fact, in A.A. Although there are no explicit laws governing such acts Dan informed Byron that A.A. had only one commodity to dispense, and that was sobriety. Giving money to derelicts would only encourage them to keep coming back to East End because word would get around that it was a good place for a "touch."

Byron brought the question up at the next discussion meeting. All the members agreed that it was not good practice to indiscriminately hand out money to beggars. However, some of the members said that there might be some extenuating cases in which the purchase of a meal or a night's lodging, or even the outright gift of a dollar or two was justified. Nobody could tell Byron just when he might properly give a person some money but apparently he was to "play it by ear." By and large, however, the practice of doling out funds for derelicts was to be discouraged.

However, these unkempt characters frequent meetings and partake of coffee and cake to their hearts' content with impunity because nobody can challenge the fact that they are alcoholics who need help. Conceivably they are bonafide participants in the A.A. program.

Shortly thereafter Byron was approached by an alert looking young man in his early thirties wearing some ragged clothing. The fellow introduced himself as Richard and said he was from Philadelphia although his family lived in New York. He wondered if he could talk to Byron personally after the meeting. Bearing in mind the Twelfth Step and realizing this was his first real opportunity to help another alcoholic, Byron readily agreed. They went to a nearby coffee shop after the meeting.

Richard told Byron that he had just been discharged from a mental hospital in Philadelphia and had come to New York to find a job. He was depressed and could not go to his family because they had become fed up with him on account of his drinking. At the present time he had only one dollar left out of five that a priest had given him and he hoped that Byron could find some place for him to sleep that night. Perhaps he might also be able to borrow a few dollars until he was able to find a job.

Byron remembered that he had been cautioned about giving away money; so he took Richard over to the Y.M.C.A. and got him a room for the night, agreeing to meet the next morning for breakfast and to map out some plans for finding a job. The next day Byron "loaned" Richard five dollars with which to buy shaving equipment and get his suit pressed so that he could find work. They agreed to meet that night at an A.A. meeting because Byron had to get to work that morning.

Richard appeared at the A.A. meeting and reported that he could not find a job. Meanwhile he apparently had had a few drinks to bolster his morale because Byron's five dollars were gone and Richard smelled like the proverbial brewery. At the A.A. meeting Byron asked a member of East End what course of action he should follow now. He was told that sometimes it was harder to say no than yes but in the long run it would be more beneficial for everybody involved.

Byron told Richard that he had no more money and that he could offer nothing more than his assistance in helping Richard get sober in the A.A. program. This did not please Richard, who claimed that his only alternative was suicide unless he could get some other means of support. Byron was adamant and refused further financial assistance. This ended their relationship although Byron did see Richard at other A.A. meetings around New York.

Because the role of a Twelfth Stepper is not precisely defined there is some disagreement as to the normative expectations. Byron's earlier behavior in giving Richard money and lodgings was disapproved of by most of his friends in A.A. to whom he told the story. However, despite the fact that they felt he had not done the right thing they told him that the best teacher in A.A. was experience and that he had certainly learned a valuable lesson.

Here, then, is a different form of deviant behavior, milder in a sense but still not resulting in any strong ridicule or punishment. It was regarded as part of a general learning experience. This supports Clinard's point that "reactions to deviations from . . . norms can vary in the direction of approval, tolerance or disapproval."[26]

So far we have only reported instances in which deviant behavior, as construed by A.A., has not resulted in negative sanctions. As in all groups there are occasions which call for the disciplining of a member for some norm violation. The nature and extent of the sanctions depend upon the means of social control available to the group. Alcoholics Anonymous has no mechanism for instituting physical sanctions, the ultimate of which is expulsion from the organization. It is also unable to mete out economic penalties so that it must rely almost exclusively upon psychological rewards and punishments.

The following illustrates a norm violation, with subsequent sanctions.

A member of East End had a serious "slip" and two of his friends went to his home when called by his wife. The member, Frank, was in bad shape. His wife said he had not eaten for a few days and that she would like to put him in the hospital. However, Frank had already been to Town's Hospital twice so that he could no longer gain admittance there, two trips being the maximum. It was decided that they would have to drive Frank to a private rest home in Connecticut, about a three-hour trip from New York.

One of the Twelfth Steppers, Mel, had a car and it was agreed that they would all drive up together. The problem was that Frank was in no condition to travel because he was almost completely unconscious. It was agreed that they would take turns watching Frank and as soon as he sobered up sufficiently to be able to navigate they would leave.

Mel's colleague said he could spend the night with Frank while Mel went home, and that by morning they should be able to make the trip. The following morning Mel called and said that he had a sudden urgent business call and would not be able to drive up to Connecticut, nor could he loan them the car for the journey.

Mel's partner was upset by this. He and Frank's wife spent two hours on the telephone until they found another member who had a car and who would take them to the rest home. Word got around in the group that Mel had backed out of a Twelfth Step commitment and there was a considerable amount of gossip about this infraction of an important obligation. Gossip is one of the chief forms of social control, although it too is ostensibly discouraged in A.A. circles.

The case of Elsa also illustrates some negative aspects of deviancy.

Preparatory to selecting a slate of officers to serve for a six-month period, the East End group chooses a three-man committee to recruit the best possible candidates. This usually involves a lot of telephone calling between the members of the nominating committee and potential officers to ascertain their availability. The opinions of all the group members are also solicited.

Elsa was being considered for the post of secretary but somebody informed the nominating committee that she had had a recent "slip," which would have made her ineligible for office. The story was completely untrue because Elsa was a thoroughly reliable and sober member who had not had a drink since joining A.A. two years earlier. Elsa heard of the report of her "slip" and was very disturbed by such a wild tale. She was particularly upset because she said she thought that the people in the group had more faith in her than to believe that first of all she would drink and secondly that she would not tell them if she had. The person who originated the rumor was told by others that Elsa was fuming. As a result this individual stayed away from East End for a few meetings until she had a chance to explain to Elsa how the misunderstanding had developed.

One further case illustrates a rare example of direct criticism of a member.

Hilda had been a member of East End for about a year when she was elected secretary. She was relatively new in A.A. and expressed some anxiety about her ability to perform the duties of the post. The group assured her that she would do fine. For the first month Hilda discharged her responsibilities adequately.

One night at an open meeting an East End member with whom Hilda had a strong friendship came to the meeting with a brand new "pigeon." The member introduced the "pigeon" to Hilda and the meeting got under way. During the secretary's break for announcements Hilda very proudly introduced the new "pigeon" to the assemblage and asked for some applause to show the neophyte that she was most welcome. At the conclusion of the meeting several East Enders told the chairman that he ought to tell Hilda to "shut up," and not to break anonymity that way. Almost the entire membership was disturbed by this unprecedented act on the part of Hilda. One member told her directly that "this is not a vaudeville show and you do not introduce celebrities nor do you ask for applause." Hilda was completely shaken by this experience and reported that she was upset and unable to sleep for a few nights thinking about the incident. At the next meeting she wanted to resign as secretary but the group told her to forget it and to continue in the position.

The above case illustrates sharp and rather severe criticism which is seldom expressed overtly in A.A. Hilda had violated the cardinal principle of anonymity by introducing a new person by her full name to a group at an open meeting, despite the fact that many speakers announce their own full names. She had also committed an infraction by the unprecedented request for applause as a sign of support for the beginner. Nevertheless her resignation was rejected and the group offered excuses for her by saying that she was inexperienced.

These illustrations represent a modicum of norm infractions and consequent reactions. A variety of behaviors fall within the category of deviancy and the responses elicited depend upon the interpretation of the severity of these violations. A listing of such acts will indicate the range of nonconforming conduct. Immediately following is an explanatory discussion of each item. The classification is in descending order of gravity as evidenced by the intensity of the manifestation of social control.

1. Attacking the A.A. program.
2. Taking the first drink.
3. Commercial exploitation of A.A.
4. Sexual advances toward female beginners.
5. Personal dishonor.
6. Inexpedient advice to beginners.
7. Refusing a Twelfth Step call.
8. Not attending meetings.
9. Failure to appear at a speaking date.
10. Professing a disbelief in a God or a Higher Power.
11. Taking another person's inventory.
12. Refusing to accept an office.
13. Refusing a speaking engagement.
14. Speaking too long at meetings.
15. Not observing A.A. etiquette.

1. *Attacking the A.A. program*

As might be expected, the subject of therapeutic devices for alcoholism is a major topic of discussion at closed meetings and informal gatherings. Invariably a comparison is drawn between A.A. and the traditional forms of psychiatric and psychotherapeutic treatment. A number of members had undertaken psychoanalysis prior to joining A.A. and for the most part the consensus is that psychiatry and psychoanalysis have failed as techniques for treating alcoholics.

The Deviant Deviants

Members of A.A. who have achieved a degree of sobriety consider themselves experts on the subject of alcoholism. No professional training is considered the equivalent of having been a hopeless alcoholic and then recovering through the A.A. self-help method. Criticism is often leveled at other practices and practitioners in the field whose course of action in dealing with alcoholism differs from that pursued by A.A. These critics point out that no other method has been as successful in coping with this problem. Alcoholics Anonymous estimates that fifty per cent of the people "make it" on first contact with the association and another twenty-five per cent follow suit at some subsequent date. As pointed out earlier, these figures are totally unsubstantiated.

A member who suggests that A.A. is not as effective as maintained and who implies that some improvements might be made in the program will be censured when broaching these ideas. The A.A. program is deemed infallible whereas other methods are considered to be less than perfect.

Alcoholics who have tried to recover through psychiatry and have failed are offered as evidence of the inadequacy of the technique. Psychiatry, as a discipline, is considered incapable of coping with alcoholism. However, when an alcoholic attempts recovery in A.A. and fails, the burden of responsibility is shifted to the individual and the program itself remains inviolate. Continuation of drinking during A.A. affiliation is an indication that the person has not applied himself to the program. It is felt that more diligent attention to A.A. prescriptions would inevitably lead to complete abstention. In other words, when the alcoholic does not achieve sobriety through psychiatry the technique is at fault, when similar lack of success is reported of A.A. then the individual, not the method, is deficient. This is indeed the best of all possible worlds.

This doctrine of absolute faith in the program is a strong factor in the therapeutic process. The alcoholic coming into the fellowship is encouraged to believe that his chances for sobriety are maximal, that the system cannot fail if only he stays with it and adheres to the format. The newcomer is presented with a body of incontrovertible evidence to this effect in the form of the group members who have conquered their drinking compulsion.

Attacks against this infallibility are intolerable. One must also bear in mind that A.A. involvement implies lifelong dedication, and such participation does not readily brook detraction.

2. *Taking the first drink*

This is obviously a grave infraction of the norms yet the sanctions are not usually negative. The anticipated response to such behavior is sympathy and assistance.

This violation falls into two categories. There is the alcoholic who has come into A.A. but who has not yet been able to stay sober, and there is the member who has achieved sobriety but has had a "slip." In both cases the individual is extended the support of the group. A member who criticizes a person for not being able to stay sober is himself committing a deviant act.

There is one East Ender who has been affiliated with the group for nine years yet his longest uninterrupted period of sobriety has been three months. Nevertheless the group does not chastise him. The feeling is that he is at least trying to stay sober and the fact that he keeps coming to meetings is evidence of this. Additionally it is felt that he would certainly have been much worse off if he had not kept in touch with the group. The only time he is subject to criticism is at discussion meetings when he offers some suggestions on how to stay sober. A person having difficulty himself in accomplishing this goal is not in a position to hand out advice on the subject. Members are not inclined to go along with the idea of "do as I say not as I do."

A female newcomer was not able to attain three months of unbroken sobriety until she had been in A.A. for over a year. During this time she came to meetings with liquor on her breath and seldom seemed to be taking the program seriously. Nevertheless her sponsor never lost patience and the group extended her every possible consideration. Ultimately the girl did succeed in overcoming her problem and now has two full years of sobriety to her credit.

In the case of the member who has a "slip" after a period of sobriety the major concern of the group is that he comes back to A.A. as soon as possible so that the damage, both psychic and physical, will be kept to a minimum. The drinker is encouraged to return to the fold and to overcome any feelings of shame or remorse that he may have.

The nature of such deviancy is quite serious; yet the group reacts in an affirmative fashion. An underlying reason for this is the strong emphasis placed on the concept of alcoholism as a disease which is difficult to arrest. Additionally, as in many other illnesses, relapses do occur. The alcoholic is thus relieved of his burden of guilt for his drinking. His "slip" is regarded as a relapse and the remedy is an extra dose of support and guidance, not castigation. Group solidarity is enhanced by dealing with such deviant behavior in the prescribed manner.

3. *Commercial exploitation of A.A.*

The A.A. program is not to be used for monetary gain. Alcoholics Anonymous does not operate any hospitals or institutions nor does it directly support any other outside enterprise. Its services are free to anyone who has a drinking problem and who wants to be helped.

The following case is an illustration of a flagrant breach of this norm.

Robert is about fifty-five and has been in A.A. for two years. He is an attorney and is apparently quite wealthy.

Robert first called on A.A. for help when he realized that his drinking was completely out of control. At his first meeting he met a member who claimed he had been sober for four years. This person told Robert that he would be glad to be of assistance and would like to help in any way possible. Robert was impressed by this expression of friendship and soon relied upon the member for advice and support.

Shortly thereafter Robert had a severe drinking bout and his new-found friend suggested hospitalization. Robert agreed and during his five days in the hospital his A.A.

colleague visited daily, spending as much as three hours at a time with him.

When Robert was released from the hospital he remained at home for two weeks to recuperate. During this period he was visited daily by his comrade. However, the friend now told Robert that he was broke and would like a "loan" of $200 to tide him over. It was insinuated that the services rendered certainly were worth more than the sum requested. Robert was not familiar with the A.A. codes about such behavior and gladly gave the man the money which was never returned.

Recently when Robert reported this to another group member he was told he should never have given money for A.A. help, that it was contrary to the basic traditions of the program. It was suggested that Robert ask for the return of his money but he has been unsuccessful in this. The person who accepted the money was told that this was not the way A.A. operated, and that he ought to return the funds. As a result of this he left East End and transferred to another group.

Occasionally a member will charge for "expenses" involved in making a Twelfth Step call but he will usually become quite unpopular with the group if he continues such behavior. Some A.A.'s have opened private rest homes for alcoholics. Still others have found employment in large corporations as counselors and advisors on the problem of alcoholism. Such activity is not considered professionalization of A.A. and accordingly is not frowned upon so long as the individual does not say he represents Alcoholics Anonymous.

When an alcoholic, acting as a member of A.A. and participating in the program, decides to profit from such activity then he is considered to be deviant. Negative sanctions are imposed but it must be remembered that expulsion from the group is not possible so that more subtle devices must be utilized.

4. Sexual advances toward female beginners

One of the questions frequently raised at discussion meetings pertains to whether or not male A.A.'s should go out on Twelfth

Step calls from female alcoholics. The vast majority of members feel that this would be an unwise procedure. It is felt that the female alcoholic is in a particularly vulnerable position and there is no need to complicate matters by having a male member of A.A. act as her "sponsor." Additionally, it is easier for a female to identify with the problems of a woman drinker so that recovery may be facilitated.

There is no doubt that part of the attraction of A.A. is its "co-ed" make-up. A number of marriages have occurred between A.A. members. However, such emotional entanglements are not encouraged because an unhappy romance might lead to a return to drinking. Nevertheless such affairs do occur overtly and in some cases covertly. In some cases a male member may concentrate on "helping" female alcoholics who are new to A.A.

One member of East End has such a reputation. When a female new to the group appears on the scene, he is always the first to offer his assistance, usually in terms of an exchange of telephone numbers. The lady members of East End have long since become alert to his machinations and they watch him carefully. As soon as he is seen talking to a female newcomer one of them will quickly move into the discussion and take over. The entire group knows of his predilection for women and they take every possible precaution to see to it that no female unwittingly associates with him.

5. *Personal dishonor*

There are a number of ways in which dishonor may be manifested.

1. Embezzling group funds.
2. Falsifying length of sobriety.
3. Drinking but not reporting this to the group.

On rare occasions a group's treasurer will get drunk and spend the money in his trust. At best the financial records of most groups would hardly meet the most elementary accounting standards; so petty pilfering is relatively simple to perform.

When this happens the group shrugs off the loss and starts over again. If it can be definitely proven that a member dissipated group funds, he may be asked to make restitution. However, such deviant behavior may also be regarded as a symptom of the illness of alcoholism. Most A.A. members have resorted to much worse than petty thievery to buy a bottle and therefore they can fully understand a person's taking money for this purpose. This is not to say that they condone such behavior, but at least they do identify with and are not quite so disturbed by it.

Lying about drinking to maintain one's status in the group is also understandable and no dire consequences follow. However, if the person is holding office under false pretenses (minimum three months' sobriety), he will be asked to resign.

6. Inexpedient advice to beginners

The norms here are not rigidly defined. The "old-timers" have considerably more experience in guiding new people along the road to sobriety and they are usually looked to for advice when the situation warrants it.

On occasion an inexperienced member will be asked for a recommendation concerning some course of action. The professed advice may not seem too judicious to an older, more experienced member and this may be pointed out to the participants. A rather humorous incident illustrates this.

Peter, in A.A. two years, received a Twelfth Step call on a Sunday. When he could not locate another available East End member he decided to go alone. Upon arriving at the house of the alcoholic who had called for help he determined that hospitalization was required. The alcoholic agreed, although still quite drunk, and was loaded into Peter's car for the trip.

About halfway to the hospital, the inebriate, who was in quite a stupor until this point, suddenly awoke and demanded a drink before he was put into the hospital. Peter refused him the liquor despite the protestations of the alcoholic who insisted that it was A.A. custom to give a man a final drink before putting him in the hospital. Peter told him to keep quiet and they finally arrived at the hospital where appropriate arrangements were made.

Subsequently Peter recounted his experience to an older A.A. member who told him that it was indeed the custom to give a man a double shot before finally hospitalizing him, if he asked for it.

There are countless situations which arise in the course of A.A. activity which must be resolved on the spot without recourse to a manual of directions or a book of rules. Experience is the highly regarded guide in resolving these problems and the expertise of the A.A.'s in dealing with these dilemmas is most impressive.

Although there may not be complete agreement about the most propitious behavior for an alcoholic under all circumstances, experienced A.A.'s do offer practical solutions to a number of vexing problems. A member not familiar with the conventional or traditional way of resolving certain issues may offer inadvertent advice to another A.A. and will often be rebuked by an "old-timer." Such controversies are often aired at discussion meetings.

Some specific cases illustrate this point.

1. Frank was relatively new in A.A. and went on a Twelfth Step call to a hospital to pick up an alcoholic who was being discharged. On the way home from the hospital the alcoholic asked Frank if it was necessary to attend a meeting that same night. Frank told him that he did not think it too important and that a few days rest might be more suitable. When Frank reported this incident to some of the group members he was told that he had not acted wisely. An alcoholic coming out of a hospital should get to a meeting immediately and should maintain such attendance regularly.

2. During an after-meeting coffee discussion a new member asked Jack for some advice. Jack had been in A.A. for eleven months and felt quite secure in his sobriety. The newcomer had been out of a job for several months and

had finally been able to find a position as a part-time bartender. He was supposed to start work the next day and asked Jack if this would be harmful. Jack told him that the important thing was that he had found work and that even though he had to spend his time in a bar no damage would occur if he was careful. A few other members overheard these remarks and they told the newcomer that under no circumstance should he accept employment in a place where he would be around liquor all day. Although it was true that the job was vital nothing transcended sobriety in importance and the newcomer was dissuaded from reporting for that specific position. He subsequently found other work in a less threatening environment. Jack was told to check with more experienced people before he made any similar suggestions.

7. *Refusing a Twelfth Step call*

Twelfth Step work or "carrying the message" is a keystone of the A.A. program. All alcoholics in A.A. are expected to come to the assistance of others as part of their own therapy as well as a way of spreading the word that there is hope of recovery. This is looked upon as a solemn undertaking which takes precedence over any personal activities or plans which may have to be modified or cancelled.

Theoretically an A.A. is thus "on call" seven days a week, holidays not excepted. Nevertheless some members evade this responsibility by saying that they are not good at such calls, that they are ineffective or that they do not feel sure enough of themselves to take on such assignments.

In many cases refusal of a Twelfth Step call is justified, but in other instances there is no reason for such unwillingness except personal discomfort or inconvenience. This is especially true on Sundays or holidays when the member may want to relax and not be disturbed. For the most part the response is quick and affirmative but some group members have become known as reluctant Twelfth Steppers and are asked only in emergencies because they never volunteer. Such members do not merit high esteem in the group.

8. *Not attending meetings*

There are no minimum attendance requirements to maintain membership in a group. No official rosters are kept and absenteeism is not formally noted. Some members attend meetings with a fair degree of regularity while others appear infrequently.

Obviously the group could not survive if attendance declined steadily, so that some form of social pressure is exerted on those with poor attendance records. Such a person is the object of caustic comments when he finally does appear at a meeting. He will be "kidded" by some while others will tell him that he is looking for trouble by staying away from meetings. If he should offer some remarks at a discussion meeting a few members will comment that "for a guy who doesn't come to meetings he sure is quick with advice."

On the other hand there is concern for a person who suddenly stops coming after a fairly extensive period of regular attendance. Several members will call his residence or business to find out if he is well. They will tell him that he was missed the last couple of times and extract from him a promise to come to the next meeting. If he should fail to appear he will receive another barrage of calls checking on his whereabouts.

9. *Failure to appear at a speaking date*

East End, like all other A.A. groups, sends teams of speakers to other groups for their open meetings. Leaders are also provided for closed meetings and discussions at institutions.

At a closed meeting only one alcoholic leads the discussions; therefore if the volunteer doesn't arrive a substitute must be recruited at the last minute. The same holds true at institution meetings, but here the failure of a member to appear is even more serious because the patients or inmates cannot fill in for the missing discussant.

For open meetings three or sometimes four members volunteer as a team. In such a case if one speaker does not show up the others can talk a little longer to fill out the program. Despite the fact that one absence in such a situation is not too important the member will be reprimanded. He will certainly be told that he is expected to keep such appointments and if he cannot do so he should not make the commitment.

When a person does not fulfill his obligation at a closed or institution meeting the program chairman will be notified to that effect. In this situation the offender will be told that he disappointed the people waiting for him and he also spoiled the reputation of the East End group. He will be advised that the group is proud of its record of reliability and that it will soon be ruined by those who have no regard for their responsibilities.

10. *Professing a disbelief in God or a Higher Power*

A.A. officially avers that it does not have traditional religious ties although it is a "spiritual" program. God is interpreted by each individual as he sees fit. Nevertheless there are few professed atheists in A.A. This may be accounted for by the conversion of those alcoholics who claimed to be atheists when they first came into A.A. and who have had their religious beliefs reinforced by the "miracle" of their sobriety. On the other hand it may be that most non-believers find the religious overtones of A.A. unpalatable and therefore do not affiliate with the fellowship. There is no doubt that some influence is exerted on those members who openly maintain their disbelief in a Higher Power.

At discussion meetings many suggestions refer to prayer as a means of help in time of need. The spiritual aspects of the program are stressed and the word God is used frequently during discussions and talks. The individual who disagrees with such points of view learns to modify his position or remains silent in his dissent.

Every A.A. meeting, closed and open, is concluded with the recitation of the Lord's Prayer. As the meeting draws to an end the leader will say, "We will close the meeting in the usual way," or "Will all those who care to join me in the Lord's Prayer." At this point the entire assemblage rises and voices the Prayer in unison.

In the many meetings this writer attended he has never seen anybody remain seated during this ritual. In other words the response to the invitation to pray is unanimous. The author asked one professed non-believer why he stood up and mumbled the Lord's Prayer with the group. He replied that he did not want all those people staring at him. It is difficult to be a lone dissident.

11. *Taking another person's inventory*

In principle there is a prohibition against gossip in A.A. Although this norm is rather ineffective at least the members know that they are not supposed to discuss other people's conduct or be critical of someone else's behavior. Such deportment produces a feeling of guilt which results in certain kinds of rationalization.

At discussion meetings the point is frequently made that A.A.'s should not take other people's inventory and some members ask why this violation of an A.A. norm is so prevalent. The stock answer is that A.A.'s are only people subject to all the human frailties. Additionally, it is countered that when A.A.'s are talking about somebody, and perhaps criticizing him, it is not done with malice but actually indicates deep concern for the individual. As such it is a positive and helpful form of behavior. On occasion some gossip will come to the attention of the individual involved and tension may flare up in the group as a consequence. The person feels doubly maligned because A.A.'s are expected to be above such behavior.

12. *Refusing to accept an office*

Because of the relatively large number of offices which must be filled every six months, most members are requested to serve in some capacity sooner or later. Some individuals do not feel qualified to accept even the slightest responsibility and they decline. Others do not want to extend themselves beyond minimal participation and they too refuse. This reduces the field considerably and sometimes makes it difficult to present a full complement of officers.

The group is generally quite sympathetic toward those alcoholics who legitimately claim that they are not ready for extra duties. However, a dim view is taken of those who are only shirking their obligations. Such persons become the object of negative comments.

> Ellen has been a member of A.A. for six years but has never held office. She is quite vociferous in her complaints about the way the group is being run and never fails to let the office holders know that things could stand improvement. One night she grumbled about the lack of proper coat checking facilities. A member became angered at this and told her that she ought to become a little more constructive in her activity. Because she had refused an office each time it was offered the least she could do now was to refrain from criticism and let those people who were more conscientious run things to the best of their ability.

13. *Refusing a speaking engagement*

All members are urged to participate as speakers at outgoing meetings. Such opportunity is readily available for those who wish to enter into such activity. Occasionally there will be a shortage of volunteers and the program chairman may then ask a member if he or she is free for a specific date.

Some members are reluctant to address large gatherings while others may not want to give up their leisure time. If a member refuses a speaking date two or three times he will be removed from the list of potential volunteers and will not be asked to offer his services. His status in the group will be lowered by this lack of cooperation.

14. *Speaking too long at meetings*

There are two ways in which this infraction of the norms may occur:

1. Taking more than one's allotted time when speaking at an open meeting.
2. Speaking beyond the unofficial but traditional 10:00 P.M. deadline.

The Deviant Deviants

When a speaking team visits another group usually three or four members participate. This means that each speaker is allocated fifteen to twenty minutes. Every now and then one of the speakers will get carried away and consume a full three-quarters of an hour for his story. The result is that one member will be excluded entirely from the program. After giving up an evening and traveling some distance, there is keen disappointment on the part of the eliminated speaker. The other members also feel that it is not fair for one person to take all the time for himself.

The speaker who has taken the excess time always apologizes profusely while the other members politely assure him that no harm was done. However, among themselves they agree that it was most inconsiderate. Three members of East End have the reputation of being long-winded, and as a result when they are scheduled to speak some people stay away from the meeting.

Florence is an old-timer in East End but has the habit of talking endlessly at open meetings. At one meeting she was scheduled to appear on the program with two other speakers, one of whom was a visitor from Chicago. Florence was the second speaker that night and managed to talk for forty minutes, allowing no time at all for the guest from Chicago. During this rambling discourse the audience was becoming uncomfortable and some members actually left the meeting in disgust at this lack of consideration. Many members were privately displeased. When the meeting was concluded Florence expressed her sincere regret to the guest from Chicago who reassured her that he enjoyed her story very much and really preferred listening to speaking. Although most of the group was unhappy a number of members expressed the opinion that Florence probably had a need to speak for that long a time and it must have done her a great deal of good.

By tradition all A.A. meetings terminate at 10:00 P.M. At one closed meeting a speaker aptly declared, "The mind can absorb only what the seat can endure." When sessions go beyond the deadline the participants tend to become restless.

15. *Not observing A.A. etiquette*

A pattern of etiquette has developed at A.A. meetings, non-observance of which results in some mild criticism.

It is customary that new people or strangers be greeted and made welcome by the members of the group. Occasionally, at a discussion meeting, the group will be called to task because it has not been hospitable and strangers have been left to themselves at meetings.

It is also considered good manners to thank the visiting speakers and to commend them for a "wonderful meeting." On occasion East End speakers have traveled to other groups for open meetings and have reported that not a single person even said "thanks for coming." Such breaches of etiquette lower the esteem in which groups are held by members of A.A.

CHAPTER EIGHT

Organization Therapy

In essence the entire program is an ameliorative device, and participation by the alcoholic in any phase of the organization's activities is theoretically an integral part of his recovery and rehabilitation. As a therapeutic agency Alcoholics Anonymous is intrinsically distinctive. It has usually been categorized as a form of group psychotherapy; yet it transcends the orthodox forms of treatment in certain respects. Alcoholics Anonymous is fundamentally "organization therapy" involving the structure and processes of the total social system of the association.

Group psychotherapy is defined as "processes occurring in formally organized, protected groups and calculated to attain rapid ameliorations in personality of individual members through specified and controlled group interaction. . . . Psychotherapy is a formal, not an incidental process. It is not the resultant of other primary activities. Psychotherapy is the primary activity."[1] Implicit is the notion that this formal procedure is under the direction and supervision of a trained, professional therapist.

However, A.A. emerged and expanded without the specific guidance of psychiatrists, psychologists, or other members of the healing disciplines. Bacon rightfully indicates that "the rise of the phenomenon of A.A. can be traced directly to the trial-and-error tactics of a small group of alcoholics trying to help themselves."[2] Practical, painful experience provides the basis for direction and guidance. Every recovered alcoholic in the program has lived through the same episodes which the still suffering drinker is undergoing. Identification between active alcoholics and A.A. members is realistic and tangible. The members of the program are living proof that "it can be done."

The desire to stop drinking is a fundamental prerequisite to recovery. This involves the drinker's acknowledgment that his life is being seriously disrupted by his uncontrolled use of liquor. Admitting to being an alcoholic is an advantage in the program. As Clinebell points out: "This attractive in-group [A.A.] is open only to alcoholics. Joe's reluctance to admit he is an alcoholic is counterbalanced by the fact that this admission is his ticket to enter the group. His chief liability is now an asset."[3]

Jerome Frank offers an outline of group factors in the therapeutic setting which provides a paradigm for evaluating the techniques of Alcoholics Anonymous. He states that the group provides five basic functions to the therapeutic process. They are (1) permissiveness, (2) support, (3) stimulation, (4) verbalization, (5) reality testing.[4]

1. *Permissiveness*

Most neurotics suffer from too stringent internalized controls in the form of feelings of guilt and fear of others' censure which blocks self-realization, so that in the first instance the psychotherapeutic situation must convey to them a feeling of permissiveness. Permissiveness . . . is enhanced by the safety of the group situation.[5]

We have already commented upon the extent and consequences of permissiveness in Alcoholics Anonymous. It is a fundamental aspect of the program, turning guilt and anxiety into assurance, confidence, and dignity. This is basic to the reversal of status, from rejected inebriate to accepted alcoholic member of A.A.

2. *Support*

Permissiveness must be accompanied by some sort of guidance for the patient as he attempts to explore and modify his attitudes. . . . Support is also necessary to combat the paralyzing loss of self-confidence from which many emotionally ill patients suffer. The therapeutic group is actively supportive in its members' efforts to understand and appreciate rather than judge each other. A patient's morale may be strengthened simply by feeling himself a member of such a group, sharing its goals and standards and believing in the efficacy of its methods. A patient may be encouraged by seeing others improve and his self-esteem may be enhanced by the knowledge that he is helping them. Demoralizing feelings of difference and isolation are combatted by the discovery that one's feelings and problems are shared by others, and by finding oneself taken seriously by one's peers.[6]

Almost every activity in A.A. is designed to offer support to the alcoholic. The norm against "taking somebody else's inventory" is an attempt to limit critical appraisal of another individual's conduct, past or present. The A.A. member does not stand in judgment but extends his sympathy and understanding.

The Twelve Steps are a guide toward individual recovery. Additionally, any member of A.A. who has achieved some length of sobriety is available for consultation as to "how to do it." As soon as the new member is able, he will find his own status enhanced by the opportunity to be of assistance to other drinkers worse off than he. Self-confidence is immeasurably induced by this process. His own feelings of inferiority are modified as soon as the member helps another person achieve sobriety. Rather than being dependent he is now a source of strength and guidance. It is doubtful if a psychiatrist would place one of his patients in the care of another, yet this procedure is a rehabilitating factor in A.A.

The group itself is a major bulwark of support. Here the problem drinker finds a body of alcoholics who have been able to stay sober for varying lengths of time, something he has desperately desired himself. His acceptance into such a group, and his encouraged participation, is effective support for his low state of mind and his diminished self image. In this milieu he finds opportunity for psychological satisfaction and growth.

3. *Stimulation*

Neurotic responses must be expressed in the therapeutic situation if they are to be changed by it. The group stimulates such expression in addition to offering permissiveness and support. Members' feelings may be stirred up, for example, by direct contagion, by associating to the problems of others, by envy of another member's progress, . . .[7]

The above is equally applicable to A.A. At closed meetings there is overt rivalry concerning the best suggestions to the various questions raised. On occasion members directly contradict each other and spirited exchanges follow.

There is also competition regarding the extent of participation in various A.A. activities. Some members feel that they are being overlooked when it comes to Twelfth Step calls or speaking engagements, implying that others monopolize these pursuits. Specialization has also developed so that some alcoholics have achieved recognition as good Twelfth Steppers or inspiring speakers or excellent administrators. These forms of interaction contribute to the therapeutic process.

4. *Verbalization*

Since the verbal apparatus is our chief analytical tool, putting feelings into words is an important, perhaps an essential prerequisite to clarifying and changing them. The free give-and-take of group discussion, the efforts to make one's position clear, to win arguments, to respond to other's interpretations of one's behavior, and so on, often are powerful incentives to therapeutically useful verbalization. . . .[8]

In Alcoholics Anonymous this aspect of verbalization is actually built into the organization. The social norms call for participation in discussion groups, sometimes leading such sessions. Members are also expected to speak at open meetings.

At the termination of the formal phase of meetings there is the "coffee therapy" which consists of informal discussion between small groups of alcoholics. At the conclusion of these conclaves many members depart from the meeting room and reassemble at a neighborhood coffee shop for prolonged conversations.

"Nickel therapy" is a frequently used device consisting of telephone calls from various members to each other. It is highly recommended that a member who is feeling depressed or morose call another A.A. on the telephone and discuss his problems. The term persists despite the disappearance of the five-cent phone call.

The Twelfth Step is essentially a process of verbal interaction. A.A. members relate their drinking experiences and tell the inebriate how they were helped to recovery. Even during personal conversations when A.A.'s are together socially, a major part of the evening's discourse is usually concerned with some phase of alcoholism.

5. *Reality Testing*

All psychotherapeutic situations contain elements of novelty and familiarity which facilitate testing old and new attitudes and ingraining the appropriate ones through practice. The novel aspects, some of which are implied in the discussion of permissiveness, support, and stimulation, help the patient to gain new insights into his attitudes, especially when others fail to respond as he expects. The familiar aspects allow him to test his responses on the spot and transfer what he learns to everyday life. . . . This similarity to real life goes along with significant differences—for example, a permissiveness whch attenuates the penalty for failure and the relative directness and honesty of the members' reactions which help each to see how his behavior is perceived by others. These qualities make the group especially useful for testing and improving social skills. . . .[9]

Reality testing is particularly characteristic of the A.A. therapeutic process. The alcoholic comes to A.A. wanting to learn how to stay sober. Absolutely no emphasis is placed on exploring the unconscious or examining the underlying causality of the drinking behavior. The concentration is on achieving sobriety and staying away from the first drink. The therapeutic efforts are directed at accomplishing this purpose, not primarily at unearthing trauma and motives.

Because treatment is at the conscious, behavioral level there are many practical and directly applicable devices which are of considerable assistance in bringing about and maintaining recovery. The Twelve Steps are a broad guide for personal rehabilitation, but also there are a number of invaluable suggestions put forward by the "experts."

Some of the following recommendations are proposed to help the inebriate achieve and sustain sobriety.

1. Keep coming to meetings.

2. Be active in the program.

3. If you feel like taking a drink call an A.A. member and talk it over.

4. You don't have to stay sober forever, twenty-four hours at a time will do.

5. It's the first drink that gets you drunk because it leads to the tenth; so just stay away from that one drink.

6. One drink is too many and a thousand not enough.

7. Carry chocolate bars with you at all times. If the desire for a drink becomes powerful, eating a candy bar will help dispel the impulse.

8. Stay away from parties or other places where liquor is served.

9. If you have to go to such gatherings take a glass of ginger-ale. Nobody really cares what you are drinking as long as you have a glass in your hand.

10. Don't think you have to drink for business reasons. You would be amazed to learn how many people do not drink at all.

11. If your abstinence is embarrassing tell the other person that you are slightly indisposed and cannot drink today.

12. If you can't sleep don't take pills. Nobody ever died from lack of sleep.

13. Don't start thinking you are cured, you're not. Once an alcoholic always an alcoholic; so, stay away from so-called "social drinking."

14. Hang around old-timers, their experience is helpful.

15. Your sobriety comes first and anything that threatens it is to be avoided.

The organization itself provides the framework within which individual rehabilitation is effected. Alcoholics Anonymous is essentially a circular system in which the organization is the therapeutic agency and in turn is molded and shaped by the activities and accomplishments of its members.

The shared experiences of the group create for the alcoholic a closed world in miniature, a society of its own with common norms and values. Here the discrepancy he has felt between his own needs and practices and the demands of the larger outside world disappears. In this social order all inhabitants are problem drinkers and there is no need to suppress feelings of guilt and remorse. Status in the organization is accorded the alcoholic for the behavior which formerly resulted in condemnation. The feelings of inadequacy and rejection brought about when an individual is isolated from the general society are overcome.

During talks at open meetings and discussions at closed sessions the alcoholic is able to bring into the open the sordid details of his drinking history. No act of deviance is considered too perverse for frank enunciation. The norms of the group implicitly and explicitly relieve any guilt he may harbor about his past behavior. He is made to feel that a new way of life is commencing and that in fact he has been reborn. There are "birthdays" and "anniversaries" which are commemorated in the program, marking the inception and length of sobriety.

The alcoholic is now a member of an extremely selective in-group. Additionally, as soon as he has achieved three months of sobriety he qualifies as an "expert." He possesses knowledge which is not available to outsiders and he is entrusted with the responsibility of helping other alcoholics. He has the know-how to do this and finds himself in a superior position compared to "civilians" who never had the problem and to other alcoholics who have not been able to stop drinking. The fact that some members had formerly been treated by psychiatrists or had unsuccessfully sought help in their churches reinforces faith in the A.A. way. For the most part religion and psychiatry have not been successful in rehabilitating the problem drinker. The achievement of sobriety in A.A. and the ability of the recovered alcoholic to utilize these "skills" to help others enhances his status and augments the favorable image of the association.

As an insider the alcoholic shares in mutual confessions and feels responsible for the secrets which have been entrusted to him. His advice and companionship are solicited. The formerly lonely, isolated social deviant now finds himself part of a viable fellowship. The encouragement of informality and congeniality, the almost exclusive use of first names, the sense of sharing a common problem and achieving a solution through mutual assistance increase the individual's social solidarity and the organization's cohesion.

The most important aspect of "organization therapy" is the socialization process which leads to A.A. as a "way of life." The "sponsor"-"pigeon" relationship is a reincarnation of the father-son pattern of former years. The characteristics of a primary group are developed in the A.A. unit. Members intimately interact in all phases of everyday affairs. They dine together, go to shows together, talk together, and generally spend much of their free time in each other's company.

The relative permanence of these relationships is attributed to a basic A.A. principle. The members are advised that they are never to consider themselves cured, that their illness has merely been arrested. The goal of the organization is not to aim for a cure but to prevent relapses from occurring. The organizational requisite is thus perpetuity, a factor which has many implications for its structure and development.

Among the significant factors in A.A. effectiveness is the charisma of the founder Bill W. Bill is a revered leader whose books are read and whose word is quoted as gospel. However, for an organization which strives to perpetuate itself there is an inherent danger involved in the ultimate passing from the scene of the charismatic head. Provisions have been made to prepare for such an eventuality. The publication of the "Big Book" and other A.A. scriptures afford a written legacy of A.A. traditions and procedures. The emergence of a large-scale bureaucracy is part of the general plan for the continuation of A.A.

However, with the development of such a bureaucracy certain difficulties may be anticipated.

One such problem pertains to financing an expanding organization. A basic A.A. principle is financial independence. Each local group is self-supporting and is autonomous in this respect. This is also considered to be of therapeutic value to the alcoholic, indicating the way in which organizational and individual activities are interrelated. For the alcoholic there is considerable pride in being self-sufficient. During his drinking days he was frequently without funds and was certainly a poor credit risk. He now belongs to an association which actually refuses outside economic assistance. This is all the more rewarding in the face of the countless fund drives which he observes in the larger society.

The national organization depends upon contributions from the local groups for financial support. Within the local units there are no dues or fees and all funds are raised by voluntary contributions. This is also an essential ingredient in the therapeutic process. There is no charge for affiliation so that every alcoholic, regardless of his monetary status, can avail himself of the program for recovery. There may be trouble ahead concerning financial matters as the association extends its scope and activities.

Local group autonomy has always been highly regarded in A.A. because it is at this level that the actual therapeutic process takes place. Discussion groups cannot exceed a certain size and the total membership of any unit must be limited if it is not to become unwieldy. As A.A.'s reputation has spread, the number of local groups has increased tremendously. It remains to be seen whether the proliferation of the local groups will have an adverse or favorable effect on the long-range development of the association.

Participation in Alcoholics Anonymous requires considerable involvement for the alcoholic. His A.A. affairs are of paramount importance and he finds great satisfaction in being part of the fellowship. The author has heard some alcoholics remark that they hope a cure for alcoholism is never found because they would not know what to do with themselves without A.A.

CHAPTER NINE

A.A. As a Voluntary Association

In the introduction to this volume we indicated that the emergence of an organization such as Alcoholics Anonymous was significant because it inaugurated a certain form of non-institutional, voluntary control and rehabilitation of large-scale social deviancy. It now remains for us to examine the features of the fellowship which are a consequence of the self-determined nature of its membership. We shall also compare Alcoholics Anonymous with other voluntary associations, particularly those concerned with health and welfare programs.

Virtually all voluntary associations in the United States have a democratic form of organizational structure. However, as Barber indicates, "this is the nature of the internal structure . . . and the interest it represents."[1] In other words the democratic format is intrinsic to the system but not to the requirements for admission and membership.

All associations place some limitations on membership. Sex, occupation, nationality, religion, social class, athletic prowess, political beliefs, and other criteria may be qualifications for affiliation. Some associations have stringent requirements while others have minimal restrictions. Sills, in discussing the National Foundation for Infantile Paralysis notes:

> Officially the membership of a Chapter consists of the signers of its Certificate of Organization, the members of the Executive Committee and such persons as may be elected to membership. In practice, however, the membership of the Chapter consists of the Executive Committee and a number of other people who have either been invited to join . . . or who have volunteered. . . .[2]

A.A. As a Voluntary Association

Many voluntary associations, particularly health and welfare groups, depend upon the "good citizen" for membership. In fact being a volunteer in such movements is equated with praiseworthy citizenship.[3]

The organizational structure of such associations is described by Barber:

> The democratic association is characterized by frequent and regular election of officers, short terms of office, and the rotation of any given official position among as large a number of members as possible.[4]

This format is quite typical of A.A. Local groups have elections of officers every six months. No officer may hold office for more than six months nor can any officer succeed himself. All members are encouraged to participate in these activities. The short term of office and the rules about rotation afford each person an opportunity to serve in some capacity. Additionally, most A.A. groups seldom exceed a membership of thirty, and with five or six offices to fill every six months everybody who wishes to has occasion to officiate.

With reference to requirements for membership, A.A., in many respects, is unlike any other voluntary association. In a certain sense A.A. is the most permissive type of fellowship insofar as anybody who presents himself must be admitted. No votes are taken, no initiation rites are performed and no dues are paid. There is one, and only one, specification for such membership—the individual must express a desire to stop drinking. In essence, therefore, membership is closed to the general public but is open to the social deviant—the problem drinker. In addition, because affiliation is anonymous, a member can hardly be accorded the designation of "good citizen" for such participation.

After a person has decided to join A.A. he need not affiliate with any one group but may attend meetings and participate in the program at his own discretion. Most members identify with a particular local group but this is not binding and changes may be made whenever desired by the individual. In no case may a member be expelled from a group, another singular characteristic of Alcoholics Anonymous.

Speaking of local autonomy of voluntary associations, Barber says:

> When the association is large enough to be divided into many branches, it is considered desirable to have relatively large local autonomy; a flow of power up from the local groups to the central coordinating group. In the large association, when national conventions are held, the democratic election of delegates to the conventions is valued as a means of achieving total group influence on the policy of the association.[5]

This statement aptly pertains to Alcoholics Anonymous. Each local group is relatively autonomous. There is a communication network between these units but they function independently. In addition there is little formal control exerted by the national office. It is true that occasional solicitations for funds are made through the group representative but such contributions are voluntary. No assessments are ever levied, and the national headquarters has no formal machinery for imposing sanctions. On rare occasions when a local group, or a member, flagrantly violates some cardinal principle, the national office is limited to indirect means of obtaining conformity. The following example illustrates this:

> One of our pioneer members conceived the idea of starting a group in his city by radio. The local station, with a radius of about a hundred miles, offered to help. So our promoter friend constructed a series of lectures . . . which were a strange mixture of A.A. and his own religious ideas. He soon put them on the air with all the rigor of a Chautauqua orator. Contrary to our expectations, he got a modest result. Inquiries came in and he started a group.
>
> Now flushed with success, he was smitten with a wonderful vision. He wrote Headquarters, telling how a prominent life insurance company would sponsor him on a national network. He was going to appear under his own

name, as an A.A. member. For doing such a great work, of course, he was to receive a generous fee.

We remonstrated, but it was no use. We advised him that the Trustees felt his message inappropriate for national consumption. So he wrote a stinging letter to this effect: "To hell with the trustees, the World is waiting for my message. I've got the right of free speech and I'm going on the air whether you like it or not."

This ultimatum was an alarming poser. It looked like promotion, professionalism, and anonymity-breaking all in one package. If this sort of venture proved successful, from the promoter's point of view, every ad man and salesman in Alcoholics Anonymous would soon be selling A.A.'s wares, willy-nilly.

So Headquarters took this tact: We assured our well-meaning friend that we would certainly uphold his right of free speech. But we added that he ought to uphold ours too. We assured him that if his "lectures" went on the air, we would advise every A.A. group of the circumstances and ask them to write strong letters to the sponsoring life insurance company, letters of a kind that the sponsor might not like to receive. The broadcast never went on the air.[6]

The General Service Conference proclaimed at the time of its formation in 1955:

That in all its proceedings, the General Service Conference shall observe the spirit of the A.A. Tradition, taking great care that the Conference never becomes the seat of perilous wealth or power; that sufficient operating funds plus an ample reserve, be its prudent financial principle; that none of the Conference members shall ever be placed in a position of unqualified authority over any of the others; that no Conference action ever be personally punitive or an incitement to public controversy; that though the Conference may act in the service of Alcoholics Anonymous and may traditionally direct its World Services, it shall never enact laws or regulations binding on A.A. as a whole or upon any A.A. group or upon any member thereof, nor shall it perform any other such acts of government; and, that like the Society of

Alcoholics which it serves, the Conference itself will always remain democratic in thought and action.[7]

There are a number of reasons for the emphasis on local self-government. Most important is the primary goal of A.A. to provide for the sobriety of the alcoholic. For this purpose no elaborate organization is needed, just a small number of alcoholics meeting together. Each local unit is also financially independent. This financial policy further serves to enhance immunity from national supervision and control. The historical development of the association and the loosely defined nature of its membership also contribute to the greater degree of local autonomy.

Some form of written constitution is typical of most voluntary associations. This documents the organizational structure, the precise aims of the group, and the means for accomplishing these goals. A major feature of this formulation is the specification of offices to be filled with obligations and responsibilities spelled out in detail.

A.A. has no such written constitution. Each local group does have a number of offices but there are no codified rules or regulations specifically defining the formal structure and procedures. Custom and tradition are the governing factors. The Twelve Steps and Twelve Traditions are documented for membership guidance but do not embody the force or authority of a regular organizational constitution.

This does not mean that A.A. has been entirely free of bureaucratic trends. Rose asserts that "once a voluntary association is formed it may undergo one of several processes of development. Some associations die shortly after they are created; others continue indefinitely without developing; still others have a growth in structure and function."[8] A.A. is certainly illustrative of the latter category. It is also typical with respect to the bureaucratic tendencies of such voluntary associations. Chapin described these developments:

> A group of citizens meet informally to consider some problem or need. After a few conferences a chairman is selected.

As the problem under discussion is broken down into its elements, various committees are appointed; executive, ways and means, publicity, program, survey, etc. Soon the half-time services of an executive secretary are provided. He soon finds it necessary to have a clerk-stenographer. Supplies are purchased. As the work grows in volume, it is systematized by establishing membership requirements and dues. A constitution and bylaws are adopted at some stage of its development. The organization may be incorporated. A full line of officers may be chosen. As the funds accumulate and a bank account is established, the treasurer is bonded and an annual audit is required.

Meanwhile the organization finds more office space necessary. A full-time secretary is engaged. Additional clerks are needed. Office equipment is increased by additional typewriters, chairs, desks, filing cabinets and other equipment. An office manager is chosen. As time passes, and the full-time staff grows in size, vested interests "in the job" appear. Some staff persons become more concerned with the perpetuation of their jobs and guarding their rights than in the function and purpose of the organization.

. . . Along with the expansion of staff hierarchy there goes an expansion of committees of all sorts, so that the dignity and status of office take on added prestige and social position is sought for by interested persons. As the length of line organization increases, the problems of communication between different status levels become more acute. All these tendencies are signs that point to the formalization of the organization which was originally quite innocent of bureaucratic trends and characteristics.[9]

The details are not exactly descriptive of A.A.'s growth, but the general trend has been followed. Even at the local level such tendencies toward bureaucratic structure have emerged.

In a study of ninety-one voluntary associations in the Minneapolis-St. Paul area, Chapin and Tsouderos report that "those with large memberships were found to tend toward impersonal criteria and elaboration of a code of behavior, i.e., ritual, rules for membership recruitment, while associations with small membership tend toward personal discretion."[10]

Tsouderos asserts that the loyalty of members can be stabilized when participation is regarded not merely as a means to an end but as an end in its own right.[11] This is a major emphasis in Alcoholics Anonymous. The continued sobriety of the individual to a great extent depends upon his involvement in the organization's activities.

In another respect A.A. differs from most other associations which have had some influence on American society. Rose classifies voluntary associations as being expressive of social influence groups.[12] Expressive associations are those which act only to satisfy the self-interests of their members. Social influence associations are those which wish to influence or bring about some change in the larger social order. Since social influence groups have a specific and limited purpose, they also tend to have a limited life. Since change is rapid in the United States and many social problems get solved while new ones continuously rise, the turnover in voluntary associations of the social influence type is great.[13]

Alcoholics Anonymous may properly be classified as an expressive group. Its members act to satisfy their own needs in keeping sober. Yet, on the other hand, A.A. is also a social influence group. It certainly has had a dramatic impact on a major social problem of modern times. Does this mean that A.A. will have a limited life? The National Foundation for Infantile Paralysis recently underwent a transition as the incidence of polio was impressively reduced. However, there is no equivalent to the Salk vaccine for the alcoholic nor is there hope for such a development in the foreseeable future.

Alcoholics Anonymous stresses the fact that there is no known cure for alcoholism. The organization strives for perpetuation by its insistence that the members are alcoholics who continue to suffer from an illness which has only been arrested not cured. In order to keep the disease under control affiliation with the A.A. program is conceived as a lifelong commitment.

A.A. is marked by another singular feature pertaining to the prescribed degree of participation and involvement of the members. As Sills points out, "Many people do not belong to voluntary associations, but practically everyone 'belongs' to either a job or a family."[14] Barber affirms that participation in voluntary associations is defined as being less important than obligations to the family and the job.[15] Sills notes that "participation in voluntary associations is generally a leisure-time pursuit. . . ."[16] In addition some people belong to more than one association, and as both Kenneth Boulding and David Truman have reported, this multiple membership may lead to moral dilemmas and internal conflict.[17]

None of this applies to the volunteers in Alcoholics Anonymous. One of the principal norms in A.A. is that sobriety comes before all else. Alcoholics Anonymous is perceived as a "way of life" which requires total dedication. Members are available for assistance at any time of the day or night. During discussion meetings a member will report that his family resents the amount of time he spends in A.A. Without exception he is told that his sobriety comes first and that his family should realize this. The consideration of employment opportunity is also placed in this perspective. No job should ever be taken which might result in tension and anxiety to the degree that one's abstinence is threatened. If a member's present occupation tends to be disturbing he is advised to find some other employment. Neither family, nor occupation, nor other interests transcend the primary objective of remaining sober in A.A.

The members of the East End group fraternize with each other outside of formal A.A. occasions. Most members speak with at least one other A.A. daily, and social visits are frequent. The alcoholics are more than just fellow members of an association—they actually constitute the core of primary group relations. Strong bonds of friendship are encouraged and enhanced by participation in the program. In the process of recovery members hear the most intimate details of the lives of their fellow alcoholics. Such disclosures seldom come to light in other types of associations. Although members of other voluntary groups do have a common cause, alcoholism itself is the bond in A.A. This is the pervasive force in their lives around which social interaction coheres.

The fact that the members of the organization are all social deviants and their basic purpose is to serve themselves (they are the volunteers as well as the clients) provides the foundation for the organizational structure and operations. Social control is based upon the individual's motivation to gain and maintain sobriety and his realization that this can be accomplished primarily through group acceptance and participation.

This self-help aspect of A.A. produces an effective type of proselytizing program. When a problem drinker becomes a sober member of A.A. his status is enhanced by various opportunities to "carry the message" to other alcoholics. These activities are interpreted as basic to the individual's own therapy and essential to his sobriety.

CHAPTER TEN

A.A. and the "Total Institution"

Alcoholics Anonymous is a unique system for coping with one type of large-scale social deviancy. Goffman, in a formulation which has gained prominence, developed the concept of the "total institution" as one of the traditional methods for dealing with certain forms of widespread deviant behavior.[1] In many respects A.A. is a departure from the total institution of the hospital, mental institution, and prison of which Goffman writes. This in no way implies that other means of treating aberrant conduct have not been developed and utilized. The purpose of this presentation is served to best advantage by limiting the analysis to the critical distinctions between A.A. and the "total institution." Significant sociological implications may be drawn by a comparative evaluation of the two systems.

In the "total institution" there is a fundamental division between the inmates who are isolated from regular society and the staff who are part of the outside world. Alcoholics Anonymous is not so divided. The members all share the common status of alcoholic and are fully integrated with the ongoing social order. Whereas in the "total institution" the inmate is, in effect, a ward of the organization and has all of his needs attended to, the member of Alcoholics Anonymous participates in his regular familial and occupational roles. The A.A. is motivated by the work-payment structure of our society and by the benefits of full-scale family life. This is not the case with the inmate, whose motivation is of an entirely different nature. Additionally, the A.A. maintains his personal identity while the inmate is enmeshed in collective living. Both Alcoholics Anonymous and the "total institution" aim to remodel the deviant actor, yet their structures and techniques are basically at variance.

The inmate is subordinate to the staff, such subservience being based on his ascribed status and the expertise of the supervisory personnel as well as the format of the bureaucratic structure. The A.A. member is self-supervised and is endowed with the expert knowledge necessary to effect his own rehabilitation in conjunction with his fellow alcoholics. The leaders and the followers in the organization are interdependent and are of mutual assistance.

For the inmate, life is guided by bureaucratic rules and his interests are frequently secondary to the tranquility of the overall system. Collective scheduling is not conducive to rehabilitating the inmate but is implemented as a means of maintaining bureaucratic stability. The organizational aspects of Alcoholics Anonymous are also extremely important, but the focus is on the ultimate goal of supporting the member, not the system.

The "total institution" creates and sustains a particular kind of tension between the home world and the institution world, and uses this persistent stress as a means of manipulating and managing the inhabitants. For the inmate the fact of his being "in" is related to the eventual hope of getting "out." In Alcoholics Anonymous being "in" is the very essence of survival in the "out" world. The "cure" rests on remaining within the fellowship. Just the opposite effect obtains in the "total institution" in which the activities are directed at discharging and removing the inmate after his "cure" has been accomplished.

The alcoholic voluntarily assigns himself to the association while the individual in the "total institution" is usually incarcerated against his will or at best with minimal cooperation. Standard defacement occurs for the inmate. His personal belongings are removed and he is issued an institutional uniform. His family, occupation, and educational career lines are summarily terminated and a *stigmatized* status is ascribed to him. Not only is his own identity as a unique individual erased but he must also witness similar mortification of his fellow inmates. In A.A. the members also adopt a common status, but this consciousness of kind is a positive force based upon group acceptance. The status of the recovered alcoholic in A.A. provides enrichment for the individual's ego and affords him new and creative social ties. Rather than being stigmatized, his new identity as an A.A. member is rewarding. The fact that the organizational norms prescribe anonymity provides the member with a strong "in group" feeling which strengthens the rehabilitative process.

The inmate is hardly able to escape the enveloping constraint of the "total institution." Social control is bureaucratic and based upon coercive power. There are house rules, an explicit set of formal prescriptions and proscriptions, a small number of clearly defined rewards and privileges, and a well-defined system of punishments. These factors play an important part in the culture of the inmate world. Alcoholics Anonymous is basically an informal organization with no official prescriptions or proscriptions. Participation is voluntary and the system of social control is not coercive but is based upon more subtle, psychological forces. The member comes to realize that his sobriety depends upon his conforming to the basic normative system. A return to active alcoholism is thought to be the ultimate and inevitable punishment for nonconformity.

The inmate is usually relieved of economic and social responsibilties which, particularly in mental hospitals, is claimed to be of therapeutic value. However, it might be that this concept has negative consequences. In A.A. solidarity and support are gained by just the opposite orientation. The members and the groups are economically and socially independent rather than dependent. Within the organization the focus is on self-support and maturation. The need to rely upon others, except in terms of mutual assistance in the basic problems of alcoholism, is frowned upon. The member is expected to be "on his own" at the earliest possible opportunity, and any pampering in this respect is felt to delay recovery.

There is a process which the "total institution" shares in common with A.A., although with entirely different results. The fraternization process through which socially distant persons find themselves developing mutual support and common interests is found in both A.A. and the "total institution." However, in the "total institution" the mores develop in opposition to the system whereas in A.A. the norms tend to support the organization. The special language of inmates is part of the internal system which runs counter to the established hierarchy. A.A. jargon serves to create a spirit of organizational cohesion. Essentially A.A. is a way of life within the larger social system. The "total institution" is isolated and the members await an opportunity to re-enter society.

A dominant theme of the inmate's culture is the strong feeling that time spent in the institution is wasted and that a segment of his life has been destroyed. He tends to feel that for the duration of his required stay he has been exiled from life. Within the institution very little is acquired which can be transferred to the outside world. In Alcoholics Anonymous the feeling is that life actually begins with entrance into the organization. The fellowship's activities are directed toward assisting the member to fulfill his social roles in a more meaningful and effective fashion.

In the institution a peculiar kind of self-concern develops because of such confinement. The low estate of the inmate requires that he enhance his ego by fabricating some plausible and credible reasons for his current predicament. Thus a high level of ruminative self-concern develops. This is not the case in A.A. Upon affiliating with the organization the alcoholic finds that his past behavior, as deviant and sordid as it may have been, actually serves as a badge of honor. The highest prestige in A.A. accrues to the recovered alcoholic who has had the most grievous drinking history. Rather than proclaiming their innocence, the members vie with each other in recalling harrowing and horrible experiences of the past.

The "total institution" frequently claims to be concerned with rehabilitation. The aim purportedly is to reorganize the inmate's conscience and consciousness so that he will maintain the standards and norms of the institution after he leaves the surroundings. Because A.A. norms are a persistent force in the member's daily affairs this problem is avoided. The A.A. way of life does not terminate at the doors of the meeting rooms nor is there any temporal separation from the organization. The "total institution" hopes to achieve "cures" while A.A. makes no such claims. The members are forcefully advised that they are never cured and that sobriety can only be maintained by continued adherence to the organizational norms and active participation in the system. The recidivist in A.A., the person who "slips," is not chastised upon his return to the fold but is extended group support. He is living proof of what can happen to anyone who deviates from the prescribed program.

Deviant behavior within the "total institution" elicits various forms of punishment in keeping with the essential nature of the coercive power system. Deviancy within Alcoholics Anonymous is "forgiven" and is explained as a symptom or consequence of suffering from the disease of alcoholism. The deviant in the "total institution" may be threatened with prolongation of his confinement. In other words the inmate may be kept "in" longer. The A.A. *wants* to be kept "in" because his confinement is the essence of his rehabilitation. The aberrant actor in the institution also represents a threat to the bureaucratic structure so that much of what passes for rehabilitative control is really focused on maintaining order with as little conflict and tension as possible. Social control in A.A. primarily is concerned with the recovery of the individual alcoholic, which stems from group solidarity.

Entrance into the institution implies what Goffman calls "proactive status."[2] The inmate's social position on the outside will never be quite what it was prior to confinement. The stigma attached to having been in prison or a mental institution results in a permanent negative status. Entrance into A.A. can only be granted by self-definition and admission to being an alcoholic. There is no doubt that the status of the alcoholic is still stigmatized in the larger society but the anonymity of the program is an effective device for protecting the members against outside detection. More important, however, is the fact that A.A. members spend a great deal of their social lives in each other's company and in effect form a subculture in which their status of an alcoholic has positive connotations. The patient discharged from the mental institution has no such advantage. He stands alone, without the form of group support offered by A.A.

Religious Characteristics of A.A.

When discussing their initial contact with A.A. some members indicate that they were apprehensive about the nature and extent of the religious requirements for affiliation. The following comments typify this concern: "I expected a lot of Bible reading and hymn singing"; "I thought you were some kind of fanatics"; or "I had the idea that you were a bunch of Holy Rollers." Such statements usually elicit laughter, implying that misconception of the religious aspects of the fellowship is fairly common.

Officially, and vigorously, A.A. denies that it is a religious movement. It steadfastly maintains that it is a *spiritual* and not a *religious* program. The precise distinction is seldom articulated, although considerable discussion concerning this point occurs at meetings and elsewhere. Despite the disavowal of a formal theological identity there is little doubt that A.A. does manifest many characteristics of a valid religious system. Its historical origin and contemporary organization lend support to such an identity.

As mentioned previously in Chapter One, A.A. was incubated in the original Oxford Group Movement, now known as Moral Rearmament, founded by Dr. Frank Buchman, a Lutheran minister, in 1908. Buchman was visiting England at that time, when he had a "vision" which presumably caused him to alter his personality by removing such basic defects as selfishness, dishonesty, and resentments. He decided to return to the United States to spread the word of his "revelation." Meeting with only limited success, in 1920 he returned to England where he devoted his energies to converting the undergraduates of Cambridge University. In 1921 he extended his efforts to Oxford University where he concentrated on cultivating the sons of upper-class families. It was during this period that the movement took the name Oxford Group, stirring up quite a controversy in so doing. Considerable antagonism was aroused by the implied association with Oxford University and by the confusion with the earlier Oxford Movement of Cardinal Neuman.[1]

Success came slowly to Buchman, but it did come at last. In 1924 he returned to the United States and focused his attention on students of such upper-class institutions as Yale and Harvard. Returning to England he was able to convert a number of prominent persons. Once again Buchman sailed for the United States, this time with an entourage of sixty converts to bolster his campaign. There was nothing second-rate about the organization which was being established with headquarters in no less a place than the Waldorf Astoria Hotel in New York City. Buchman's influence grew rapidly and he was able to procure the personal endorsement of several respected clergymen.

By 1938 Buchman's position was so well entrenched that the doctrine of Moral Rearmament was introduced for the purpose of resolving all domestic and international conflicts. Its adherents were increasing in an accelerated fashion, partly due to massive promotional campaigns in the United States and throughout the world.

A.A. owes much of its basic doctrine to the Oxford Group principles which set forth the following fundamentals:

1. Men are sinners.
2. Men can be changed.
3. Confession is a prerequisite to change.
4. The changed soul has direct access to God.
5. The Age of Miracles has returned.
6. Those who have changed must change others.[2]

A member of the Oxford Group must fulfill the Four Absolutes prescribed by Buchman. These are Absolute Purity, Absolute Honesty, Absolute Love, and Absolute Unselfishness. One must turn his life over to God, and God will then instruct the person concerning his future behavior. This becomes a personal, individual experience in which each disciple is changed and is subject to the will of God.

In order to reach the Four Absolutes the individual passes through five steps. First, one surrenders to God. Second, one listens to God's instructions which vary according to the needs of each individual. The third step consists of "checking guidance." The member discusses the instructions he has received from God with an older, more experienced Grouper who is able to confirm the reliability of the message. This is necessary because occasionally the new member may misinterpret God's instructions and the older member is able to correct such errors. The fourth step involves implementing God's will by making amends to other people for any harm done to them in previous times. The last step is the achievement of the ideals of the Group and sharing them with other people. This may require a kind of reciprocal confessional between a new member and a Grouper. The older member reports his own shortcomings and failings at which point the new person may join in a similar recitation. When the newcomer participates in the confessional it is felt that he has been converted. The essence of this procedure has been incorporated into the Twelve Steps of Alcoholics Anonymous.

Buchman availed himself of modern public relations techniques with full implementation of social-psychological methods of propagandization. This included the use of popular slogans such as:

SIN BLINDS AND SIN BINDS
JESUS CHRIST STILL SUITS, SAVES, SATISFIES
SUPERNATURAL NETWORK OVER LIVE WIRES
COME CLEAN[3]

The utilization of somewhat similar slogans has become an integral part of the A.A. system.

There is extensive reference to the concept of God in Alcoholics Anonymous. However, emphasis is placed upon individual definition and acceptance of the meaning of God. The

Third Step is most often cited in this connection. It reads, "Made a decision to turn our will and our lives over to the care of God, *as we understood Him.*" In the Second Step reference is made to a ". . . Power greater than ourselves. . . ." The Fifth and Sixth Steps also make reference to God, and the Seventh Step states, "Humbly asked Him to remove our shortcomings."

It is obvious that, for the most part, members identify with the traditional Christian concept of God. However, it is suggested that any symbolic representation of a Higher Power may be substituted if an individual so desires. The group itself is frequently proposed as a form of Higher Power, which may be of help in achieving and maintaining sobriety.

In his volume *Religion in Contemporary Culture,* Benson devotes an entire chapter to the subject of the power factors in religion. He offers an analysis of the functions of the Higher Power in Alcoholics Anonymous and notes:

> The effectiveness of the higher power does not necessitate a particular form which the system of power takes. Members of A.A. turn to God as they understand Him. For some members the higher power is thought of merely as A.A., the power of the group which illustrates the type of higher power Durkheim found in religion. Others think of the higher power in terms of the power of human ideals, a concept similar to that of Dewey. Still others see in service to their fellow men the power which makes possible their recovery from alcoholism. Many members merely accept orthodox theological ideas which have come to them from religious denominations without fully defining what these mean.[4]

This is reiterated in *Twelve Steps and Twelve Traditions* with the following advice to the alcoholic: "You can, if you wish, make A.A. itself your Higher Power. Here's a very large group of people who have solved their alcohol problem. In this respect they are certainly a power greater than you who have not even come close to the solution. Surely you can have faith in them."[5]

Harry M. Tiebout, a prominent psychiatrist, has this to say about the nature of religion in A.A.:

> . . . The central effect, therefore, of Alcoholics Anonymous is to develop in the person a spiritual state which will serve as a direct neutralizing force upon the egocentric elements in the character of the alcoholic. . . . It is my belief that the therapeutic value of the A.A. approach arises from its use of religious or spiritual force to attack the fundamental narcissism of the alcoholic. In other words this group relies upon an emotional force, religion, to achieve an emotional result. . . .[6]

Unquestionably many members of A.A. believe that a religious or spiritual force has been the principal factor in their recovery from active alcoholism. The achievement of sobriety is often referred to as a "miracle."

In a volume dealing with religion and Alcoholics Anonymous, a Protestant minister, G. Aiken Taylor, says:

> A.A., of course, is neither religion nor an adequate substitute for true religion. It doesn't try to be. . . . Those who know it best see it only as a living "parable" within which both liabilities and assets are religiously meaningful. A.A. represents possibly the high-water mark of a practicing "psychology of religious experience."[7]

Taylor, of course, speaks from the theological point of view and bases his evaluation of the religious aspects of A.A. on its approximation to orthodox Christianity. The major part of his analysis deals with Alcoholics Anonymous from this orientation and demonstrates many similarities between the principles of A.A. and Christian theology. He also points out some areas of discrepancy between A.A. and conventional Christianity.

> To all practical purposes, official A.A. limits its concern to this life; Christianity notes that men die. A.A. frankly admits that people are imperfect; Christianity claims to know why, and relates man's imperfection to an ultimate Norm and Authority. A.A. declares that men and women need the

help of a power greater than themselves; Christianity believes that the very nature of men and women makes it
necessary to talk about some preliminary matters—such as
forgiveness—before you can talk about help. A.A. talks
about a Supreme Being; Christianity says, Yes there is a
Supreme Being, the God and Father of our Lord Jesus
Christ. . . .

A.A. needs to realize that the Scriptures, the Sacraments
and the Sabbath are not trivial; the Church, on the other
hand, could use proof that God accompanies man to his
place of business six days a week. A.A. should remember
that besides the present there is eternity; the Church should
remember that besides eternity there is the present.[8]

However, the vital issue in the present analysis is not the
degree to which A.A. does or does not resemble Christianity.
Our object, rather, is to describe those characteristics of Alcoholics Anonymous which justifiably establish it as a religious
movement. Benson comments, "Religion is so complex and
variable that the problem of establishing a classification of
types of religious organization has been a keen challenge . . .
and has proved incapable of fulfillment."[9]

For the purpose of this presentation we need not enter into
a detailed discussion of the sociology of religion. We concur
with Nottingham who says:

From the point of view of the sociologist . . . religion
may be regarded as a cultural tool by means of which man
has been able to accommodate himself to his experiences
in his total environment; the latter includes himself, his
fellow group members, the world of nature and that which
is felt by him to transcend them all. It is this last, the direction of human thought, feeling and action to things
which man feels to be beyond his ordinary everyday experience with himself, his fellows, and the natural world,
this is, the *sacred*—that constitutes, we believe, the very
core of religion.[10]

The first phase of a religious movement is frequently dominated by its principal architect, the charismatic leader. A suc-

cessful founder must have a compelling personality and the power to attract and hold followers. The history of A.A. indicates that Bill W., and to a lesser extent Doctor Bob, have filled this role admirably.

Then, as Benson points out:

> A social or religious movement cannot long survive on enthusiasm alone. It must be organized in order to defend itself against opposition, to perpetuate itself as a stable institution. It must develop a clear-cut ideology which serves as a basis of common understanding of the aims, ideas and assumptions of the movement. It must also develop a step-by-step program for bringing its objectives about.
>
> ... As part of the system of social control in the movement, procedures are developed for educating or indoctrinating followers or prospective members.[11]

One need only review the entire development of Alcoholics Anonymous to be impressed with the manner in which it has followed the design outlined above. Even more dramatic is the A.A. commitment to another prerequisite of a religious movement.

> Most religious movements have as one of their cardinal aims the bringing of a new way of life to those who are not yet converted.[12]

The Twelfth Step is an indication of the extent to which A.A. is dedicated to converting active alcoholics to a new way of life. It is concerned with "carrying the message" to other alcoholics and is considered to be one of the most important activities in the fellowship. A.A. maintains that it is a program of attraction, not promotion. This signifies that, theoretically, the movement does not recruit followers but that active alcoholics are induced to seek out the fellowship. Nevertheless, once the problem drinker has requested assistance every effort is extended to "convert" this inebriate to the A.A. way of life. It is also obvious that A.A. is the beneficiary of considerable favorable publicity which provides it with an excellent public image and enhances its program of attraction. Once drawn into the movement, the alcoholic assumes the role of a novitiate or, in A.A. terminology, becomes a "pigeon," "baby," or "newcomer." Then the full process of socialization or indoctrination commences.

Nottingham proposes the following elements as constituting the essence of religion:

1. The idea of the sacred.
2. The emotionally charged attitudes associated with the sacred.
3. The beliefs and practices that both express and re-enforce these attitudes.
4. The sharing of these beliefs and practices by a group of worshipers, who represent a community marked by common moral values.[13]

The above paradigm provides a useful frame of reference for our further analysis of the religious aspects of the A.A. fellowship.

1. *The idea of the sacred* has its complement in A.A. sacred persons, objects, and entities. The founders, Bill W. and Dr. Bob, are revered in the movement.

The first A.A. clubhouse in the world, known as the Old 24th Street Clubhouse, has become an international shrine. In early 1960 the property on which the building stood at 334½ West 24th Street, New York City, was appropriated for a new housing project. A three-day farewell observance was arranged and the small structure was disassembled and reconstructed one block away at 440 West 23rd Street.

The program for the farewell meetings best describes the attitude of the A.A. members toward the shrine.

It is undisputed that The Old 24th Street Clubhouse has a unique spot in the hearts of members of A.A., not only in the United States but in foreign countries as well.

For almost twenty years, it has been the source of rehabilitation for thousands. It has served the program well, indeed. It has been the home of General Service Headquarters, has witnessed the beginning of Intergroup and

Grapevine Magazine and it provided a tiny room that
served as home for Lois and Bill during the lean years of
the early forties.

Today finds it still a center of constantly increasing activities. It serves as Headquarters for the General Service
Conference Committee of the Southeastern District of New
York, and provides a forum for sixteen A.A. meetings a
week.

It serves as a Mecca for A.A. visitors from all over the
world, who walk through the "Last Mile," visit upstairs, see
Bill's room (kept intact), sign the guest book and never fail
to be awed by the warm humble atmosphere that embraces
them.

Now, this cradle of A.A. is facing the problem of moving.
Its present site is marked for demolition to make way for
a new building project and the chorus of hopes from the
thousands that the Clubhouse should never get away from
A.A. has echoed throughout the program for years, and has
presently taken the form of "Save the Historic Old Clubhouse as a Living Landmark for the Future."[14]

The concept of God or The Higher Power, discussed previously, is an important characteristic of the sacred in A.A.
Alcoholics Anonymous,[15] "The Big Book," is in effect the bible
of the fellowship. Passages from the book are read at meetings
and the scripture is accepted as the final word on various issues. The volume is always prominently displayed at A.A.
sessions, usually on the lectern from which the members speak
to the assemblage.

Other sacred items are the A.A. symbol, which may also be
worn in the form of a pin; A.A. slogans which are displayed
in the meeting room; The Twelve Steps and Twelve Traditions
which usually appear on some form of scroll; and the Serenity
Prayer which is printed on a small plastic card.

2. *The emotionally charged attitude towards the sacred.* This
is essentially an inherent characteristic of the sacred. It signifies
feelings of respect, awe, and reverence which members maintain toward those elements of the fellowship discussed above.

3. *The beliefs and practices that both express and re-enforce the attitudes towards the sacred.* This aspect of religion pertains to the rituals and ceremonies of the movement. The most important of these is the A.A. meeting, which in this context may be described as a devotional service.[16] The group takes on the features of a congregation which usually conducts such services twice weekly (the open and closed meeting). These sessions most frequently take place in church buildings, commonly Roman Catholic or some Protestant denomination. This serves to enhance the sacred nature of the proceedings.

The main features of the meeting have already been described in the chapter dealing with A.A. activities. The resemblance to a religious service is apparent. The reading of the A.A. preamble; the preaching of a portion of the "Big Book"; the confessionals; the "conversion"; the taking up of a collection; the veneration of the A.A. movement; the celebration of a member's "birthday" or "anniversary"; the commemoration of the founding date of the group; and the recitation of the Lord's Prayer at the conclusion of every service are all indicative of the ceremonial affirmation of the A.A. faith.

Carrying the message by means of the Twelfth Step call further augments the religious fervor of the fellowship. Proselytizing becomes the function of all A.A. members with respect to active alcoholics who would like to be saved. Each member in a sense acts as a missionary.

4. *The sharing of these beliefs and practices by a group of worshipers who represent a community marked by common moral values.* Fundamentally, this pertains to the emergence of a religious system. A.A. cannot be classified as either a denomination or a sect nor does it have the characteristics of a cult. Having passed through the first stage of development dominated by the charismatic founder, A.A. is now in the second phase of its growth in terms of a religious movement. It has emerged as a church which may be defined as the formal organization of a group of worshipers who share common and

defined beliefs and rituals concerning the sacred objects and entities they revere. Nottingham notes:

> In this second phase, which is often precipitated by the advent of a second generation of believers, qualifications for membership are made more explicit and the lines of authority in the organization are more clearly drawn. Moreover, beliefs about the sacred person and mission of the founder are formulated as official theologies and creeds and a cult of the founder involving formal acceptance of the beliefs embodied in such creeds not infrequently supersedes a more spontaneous, personal adherence to his teachings. Furthermore, religious practices . . . gradually develop into formally prescribed rituals. If a movement successfully survives the second stage, the third is characteristically one of continued expansion and diversification. The movement becomes established and takes on a variety of organizational forms. . . . At this stage a religious movement confronts the danger of becoming a victim of its own success.[17]

This is descriptive of A.A. The dangers inherent in the transition to the third stage should not be overlooked by the fellowship.

CHAPTER TWELVE

Conclusions

This volume constitutes the first comprehensive analysis of the social system of Alcoholics Anonymous. Prior accounts of A.A. have generally originated in the field of psychiatry and have concentrated on the therapeutic features of the organization. Sociologists, too, have been preoccupied with the pathological aspects of alcoholism and have focused their attention on the rehabilitative aspects of the program. Most previous reports have lauded the zeal and dedication of the A.A. members and have rather uncritically commended the success of the fellowship. The organization and development of Alcoholics Anonymous provides us with an excellent opportunity to examine certain areas of pertinent sociological interest.

The historical beginnings of the association resemble those of many other religious and social movements. The co-founders are charismatic figures in every respect, and although Dr. Bob has passed from the scene Bill W. is still a potent force in guiding the destiny of the fellowship.

As the program has expanded the process of formalization has gained momentum. Bureaucratic tendencies have emerged in the national organization as well as in the local groups. Informal structures have developed and an internal system of social stratification has evolved.

The social system of A.A. lends support to the concept that deviant behavior must be defined in terms of the prevailing norms and values of the group. Certain acts within A.A. would not be looked upon as aberrrant by outside society yet are interpreted as deviant within the association. The converse is also true.

Conclusions

The A.A. system of social control is based upon its unique organizational structure and procedures. The association does not provide any means for imposing physical or economic sanctions, thus relying on more subtle but equally effective psychological rewards and punishments. The member is constantly reminded that his status of alcoholic is permanent, that there is no cure for alcoholism, and that his stability and sobriety depend upon his continued and enduring affiliation with the organization. The normative order is thereby strongly enhanced by a voluntary system of mutual support, the denial of which may well endanger a member's sobriety. The alcoholic is cautioned that deviancy within the fellowship is likely to result in a return to active alcoholism.

Membership anonymity also has an important bearing on the system of rewards and punishments utilized in the A.A. program. For the alcoholic such anonymity re-enforces his feeling of belonging to a rather exclusive society possessing considerable expertise in dealing with alcoholism. This in-group solidarity is further augmented by the sharing of common activities and intimate experiences. Although the membership of the organization remains anonymous, the participants take considerable pride in the highly respected image which Alcoholics Anonymous has achieved internationally.

Within the organization certain statuses carry higher prestige than others. The occupants of these positions, such as group officers, receive recognition and appreciation from other members within the system. Additionally, holders of a prestige status, or members who have earned the esteem of others, benefit therapeutically in terms of ego reinforcement.

Since the A.A. member is integrated with the larger society it is vitally important that the norms of the fellowship prevail over those of the general social system in his daily life. In this context the alcoholic must give highest priority to those factors which help maintain his sobriety and must guard against those circumstances which may threaten his stability. In this endeavor the member finds considerable support by extending his A.A. contacts into other spheres. Social interaction with other members becomes pervasive. Total involvement in A.A. as a way of life is the principal safeguard against serious breaches in the normative system of the organization. In effect, a subculture is created in which the status of alcoholic has positive connotations.

As a treatment agency Alcoholics Anonymous provides a unique system of rehabilitation which we have called "organization therapy." Although utilizing many of the techniques of orthodox group therapy, the A.A. program is marked by many singular features. Of utmost significance is the theoretical concept that all aspects of participation and organizational activity are therapeutically valuable.

We have not attempted to ascertain the actual rate of success of the A.A. program. The official estimate is that seventy-five per cent of all alcoholics who come in contact with the association ultimately achieve sobriety. There is no empirical evidence to support this claim and the writer does not foresee the possibility of obtaining more accurate data. Faith in the organization and its methods is an absolute requirement if it is to afford maximum assistance to problem drinkers. The active alcoholic must believe that the A.A. way of life is infallible and that he too can gain sobriety by religiously following the program.

A.A. may be classified as a voluntary association. However, it has a number of rather singular features which distinguish it from other similar organizations.

1. Membership is comprised exclusively of social deviants.
2. Despite the deviant nature of its membership the organization has achieved the recognition and approval of the general society.
3. Membership is anonymous.
4. Membership is self-determined (by an expressed desire to stop drinking).

5. The deviant within the group as defined by A.A. norms and values is often supported, not rejected.
6. No authority exists to expel members.
7. Identification with the fellowship is neither secondary nor segmental. A.A. is a "way of life" implying primary involvement.
8. The total organization, nationally and locally, is financially self-supporting. There are no fund-raising campaigns or solicitations from outside sources. In fact such contributions are firmly and politely rejected when offered.
9. There are no dues or fees. All contributions from the members are made on a voluntary basis. No single donation may exceed $100.
10. There is no terminal point in view for the association. The goal of the program is to help alcoholics achieve and maintain sobriety, not to cure alcoholism. The A.A. member is a sober alcoholic but he must never think he is a cured alcoholic.

In certain respects Alcoholics Anonymous is representative of most voluntary associations.

1. Membership is voluntary.
2. There is a marked tendency toward formalization and the development of bureaucracy.
3. It combines expressive and social influence characteristics.
4. It is democratic in organizational format.
5. Local groups delegate authority to the national headquarters.

It is also evident that A.A. manifests many of the characteristics of a religious movement. Its historical origins, its sacred entities and objects, its rituals and ceremonies, and its community of worshipers all lend support to this observation.

No attempt has been made to predict the eventual effectiveness of Alcoholics Anonymous as an instrument of social change.

The general societal attitude toward many forms of deviancy has been considerably modified in recent years. A.A. has played an important role in altering previous stereotypes about alcoholism and the problem drinker. The organization itself is looked upon with approval by the larger society. If being an alcoholic is debilitating, membership in A.A. offers somewhat compensatory rewards.

The A.A. program signifies an important contribution to the ultimate resolution of the problems of large-scale deviancy in our society. The "total institution" consisting of prisons, hospitals, and mental institutions does not seem to be the answer at this time. To whatever extent A.A. has demonstrated its success in dealing with one form of widespread deviancy, it is conceivable that its principles may be applicable in other areas. In the next decade many more self-help and lay organizations may emerge as important factors in coping with certain complex social problems. May it not be that the accomplishments of A.A., customarily attributed by the members to spiritual factors, reside instead in the character of the unique social organization of the fellowship?

A.A. ARGOT

ANNIVERSARY—The annual date of first achieving sobriety in A.A. Members celebrate their first, fifth, or twentieth anniversaries, depending upon length of sobriety.

A.A.'s—Term by which members refer to themselves as opposed to non-A.A. civilians.

BIRTHDAY—The date on which enduring sobriety is first achieved in A.A.

BLACKOUT—A period of time and activity which occurs while drunk and which the alcoholic cannot remember after sobering up.

CIVILIANS—Non-A.A. persons in the general population. This includes social drinkers.

COFFEE THERAPY—Informal conversations and discussions after the program of the regular meeting is concluded during which time coffee is served.

D.T.'s—Delirium Tremens.

DRY—Period of time without a drink.

DRY DRUNK—Feelings of despair and depression with accompanying symptoms of being drunk despite not having had a drink. Reported as occurring even after many years of sobriety.

DRYING OUT—Process of sobering up after a period of heavy drinking.

FLIGHT DECK—The closed psychiatric ward of a hospital.

GEOGRAPHIC CURE—Attempt to overcome a drinking problem by moving from one geographic location to another. There is a vague notion that the change of scenery will alter the drinking habit.

HIGH BOTTOM DRUNK—An alcoholic who has not been institutionalized, jailed, or hit Skid Row. He may still have his family intact, may still have his job, but nevertheless is a compulsive drinker and encounters difficulty because of his drinking.

LAUGHING ACADEMY—A mental institution.

LONERS—A.A.'s in various parts of the world where they do not have groups and so work the program alone. They usually communicate with other A.A.'s by mail.

Low Bottom Drunk—An alcoholic who has suffered most severely because of his uncontrolled drinking. Usually he has lost his family, several jobs, and has been institutionalized or jailed. He is also familiar with Skid Row.

Nibbling—Taking an occasional drink.

Nickel Therapy—A telephone call to a member of A.A. when in need of help or when depressed and a desire for a drink becomes strong.

No Souls Saved After Ten—Refers to the fact that meetings terminate at 10:00 p.m.

On The Circuit—A member who participates in a large number of speaking engagements at other A.A. groups.

Periodic—An alcoholic who has uncontrolled drinking experiences between fairly long periods of sobriety.

Pigeon—A newcomer in A.A. who places himself under the guidance of a sponsor.

Shakers Corner—A corner of a meeting room where an alcoholic in poor physical condition may sit during the session without attracting too much attention.

Sitting On My Hands—Sitting through an A.A. meeting despite a burning impulse to go out and get a drink.

Slip—Any form of drinking after a period of sobriety in A.A.

Sponsor—A member who assumes the responsibility of looking after a newcomer.

Stinking Thinking—Refers to negative, destructive thinking, usually deviating from good A.A. practice and norms. An example would be "Maybe I can have just one drink."

Taking Inventory—Self-examination of one's personality characteristics with emphasis on gaining insight into those areas which can be improved.

The Big Book—The volume *Alcoholics Anonymous* authored by Bill W. Originally printed on rather bulky stock and so termed the "Big Book."

Telephonitis—A "disease" which afflicts alcoholics who make long-winded and numerous telephone calls while drunk, usually at odd and inconvenient hours.

Twelfth Step Work—Going out on a call from an alcoholic asking for help.

PUBLICATIONS OF ALCOHOLICS ANONYMOUS

Books

Alcoholics Anonymous
A.A. Comes of Age
Twelve Steps and Twelve Traditions

Pamphlets

A.A. and the Medical Profession
A.A. for the Woman
A.A.—44 Questions and Answers
A.A.—Helpful Ally in Coping with Alcoholism
Alcoholism the Illness
A.A. Tradition—How It Developed
Correctional Officials Evaluate A.A.
Fortune Reprint—A.A.
Good Housekeeping Reprint
Hospital Administrators Evaluate A.A.
Inside A.A.
Is A.A. for You
Partners in A.A.
Q. & A. on Sponsorship
Saturday Evening Post Reprint
The Alcoholic Employee
The Alcoholic Husband
The Alcoholic Wife
The Third Legacy Manual
This Is A.A.
Tranquilizers, Sedatives and the Alcoholic
Young People and A.A.

Miscellaneous Printed Matter

Basic Fact File (A.A.'s history and structure)
Conference Highlights (highlights of yearly General Service
　　Conference)
Conference Report (full report of yearly Conference)
Cooperation Yes: Affiliation No (A.A.'s relationship to outside
　　agencies)

Hospital Directory (listing of hospital groups)
How It Works (large-type excerpt from "Big Book")
Lasker Award Citations (fine paper replica, 21½" × 14½")
Pattern Radio & TV Scripts (for use with local newspapers, radio, and TV stations)
Patterns of A.A. Hospital Cooperation (five hospital programs)
Prison Directory (listing of prison groups)
Serenity Prayer (Grapevine cover enlarged)
Set of Steps, Traditions and Prayer
Twelve Steps
Twelve Traditions
Wallet Cards (Steps, Traditions, and Serenity Prayer)
World Directory (addresses of A.A. groups world-wide)
United States & World Maps (world-wide membership)

AL-ANON FAMILY GROUP PUBLICATIONS

Books

Living with an Alcoholic

Periodical

Family Group Forum (monthly newsletter)

Leaflets and Pamphlets

Alcoholism, The Problem Brought Up to Date
Bill's Talk—Al-Anon World Service Conference 1961
Freedom From Despair (adopted from a local Family Group pamphlet)
How One A.A. Wife Lives the Twelve Steps (reprint from A.A. Grapevine)
My Mother Is an Alcoholic (For Alateens by a teen-ager)
New Help for Alcoholics (reprint from *Coronet* magazine)
One Wife's Story (by the wife of an early A.A.)
Purposes and Suggestions (introduction to Al-Anon Family Groups)
The Whys and Wherefores of Al-Anon Family Group Headquarters

Publications

Homeward Bound (for relatives and friends of alcoholics in institutions)

Operation Alateen (suggestions for Alateen groups)

To the Parents of an Alcoholic

Youth and the Alcoholic Parent

Al-Anon, You and the Alcoholic

Help for the Alcoholic's Family (reprint from *Saturday Evening Post*)

The Stag Line (a special pamphlet for men)

Alcoholism, the Family Disease (help and personal stories for wives)

How to Know an Alcoholic (reprint from *Pageant* magazine)

The Twelve Steps and Traditions (discussions from the *Forum*)

To Wives & the Family Afterward (reprint of two chapters from "Alcoholics Anonymous")

Manual for Al-Anon Family Groups

Al-Anon Family Group World Directory (one copy free annually to each group)

Fact File (public relations material on Al-Anon Family Groups and Alateen)

Mimeographed Material

1960 Long Beach Convention Al-Anon Talks

Stag Meeting

Family Group Traditions

Group Structure

How to Start a Group

Suggested Programs (types of meetings)

Suggested Welcome and Preamble to the Twelve Steps

Wallet Cards

Al-Anon Introduction, Twelve Steps, Twelve Traditions and Serenity Prayer (laminated two-fold card)

Just For Today (two-fold card)

Appendix

AL-ANON AND ALATEEN[1]

The inception of the Family Groups Movement goes back to the early days of A.A. expansion. It was apparent from the very outset that the relatives of inebriates who were groping for sobriety in A.A. were in need of support and assistance themselves. By 1941 a number of family units had evolved spontaneously. In 1949 some fifty such groups applied for inclusion in the A.A. Directory. Bearing in mind its own policy of nonaffiliation A.A. was unable to honor this request. However, in 1951 several relatives of A.A. members formed a Clearing House Committee which operated from a desk leased in the old A.A. 24th Street Clubhouse in New York City. This Committee sent a questionnaire to every known family unit and from the responses the name Al-Anon Family Groups was selected. It was decided also to adopt the A.A. Twelve Steps and Twelve Traditions as the basic guide and philosophy of the new organization.

The Twelve Steps were taken over verbatim to be utilized by the Al-Anon member as a means of providing personal stability in dealing with various problems related to alcoholism in the family. The Twelve Traditions were modified slightly to meet the unique needs of the Al-Anon movement as follows:

1. (Modified) Our common welfare should come first; personal progress for the greatest number depends upon unity.
2. (Identical with A.A.)
3. (Modified) The relatives of alcoholics, when gathered together for mutual aid, may call themselves an Al-Anon Family Group provided that, as a group, they have no other affiliation. The only requirement for membership is that there be a problem of alcoholism in a relative or friend.
4. (Modified) Each group should be autonomous, except in

matters affecting another group or Al-Anon and A.A. as a whole.

5. (Modified) Each Al-Anon Family Group has but one purpose: to help families of alcoholics. We do this by practicing the Twelve Steps of A.A. *ourselves,* by encouraging and understanding our alcoholic relatives, and by welcoming and giving comfort to families of alcoholics.

6. (Modified) Our Al-Anon Groups ought never to endorse, finance, or lend our name to any outside enterprise, lest problems of money, property, and prestige divert us from our primary spiritual aim. Although a separate entity, we should always cooperate with Alcoholics Anonymous.

7. (Identical with A.A.)

8. (Modified) Al-Anon Twelfth Step work should remain forever non-professional, but our service centers may employ special workers.

9. (Modified) Our groups, as such, ought never to be organized; but we may create service centers or committees directly responsible to those they serve.

10. (Modified) The Al-Anon Family Groups have no opinion on outside issues; hence our name ought never to be drawn into public controversy.

11. (Modified) Our public relations policy is based on attraction rather than promotion; we need always to maintain personal anonymity at the level of press, radio, TV, and films. We need to guard with special care the anonymity of all A.A. members.

12. (Identical with A.A.)

During the succeeding years the Family Group movement achieved public recognition. Many new groups appeared in the United States, and a number of units were formed overseas. The Clearing House was inundated with inquiries and correspondence just as A.A. had been in its formative period. Similarly it was found that the flood of mail made it necessary to augment the staff of volunteers with several paid personnel. In 1954 the Clearing House incorporated as a non-profit organization and assumed the name of Al-Anon Family Group Headquarters, Inc.

In 1955, a book, *The Al-Anon Family Groups: A Guide for the Families of Problem Drinkers,* was published by the association. The volume was revised and enlarged in 1960 and issued under the title *Living With An Alcoholic.* Emulating A.A. the association compiled a World Directory of Al-Anon Family Groups which is brought up-to-date annually. In addition a monthly periodical, "The Family Group Forum," is put out and one copy is sent free of charge to each group. Subscriptions are available to individual members for a nominal fee. The organization also publishes an extensive list of pamphlets, leaflets, and other tracts.[2]

Again following the example of A.A., in 1961 the Al-Anon Family Groups instituted a three-year trial Service Conference of Delegates from North America. It is hoped that this conference will become a permanent means of providing representation for Al-Anon groups throughout the world. The directors of Al-Anon Headquarters are assisted by an Advisory Board of volunteer members. All financial books are audited and reports are published regularly. Headquarters is maintained by voluntary contributions from the constituent groups. Local units are autonomous and self-supporting but are expected to donate sufficient funds for the operation of Headquarters as well as the Intergroup office.

The Al-Anon Intergroup facility functions very much like its A.A. counterpart. It compiles, revises, and distributes meeting lists and keeps a current roster of names and addresses of group secretaries. Intergroup also mails a monthly bulletin to each group, arranges program exchange meetings, and plans "new officers" meetings in June and December of each year for the newly elected group officials to meet each other. In addition Intergroup organizes an annual get-together usually held at the time of the A.A. General Service Conference. Proceeds after expenses help defray the cost of maintaining the Intergroup office. Just as in the A.A. Intergroup, the Al-Anon office is staffed by members who volunteer for desk duty, usually once or twice a month.

At the present time there are twenty-two hundred Al-Anon Groups listed in the World Directory. The movement has been growing at a rate of approximately one new unit per day, with six hundred groups added last year while two hundred dropped out for various reasons. Because the majority of alcoholics are males, Al-Anon membership is preponderantly female, consisting mostly of the wives of problem drinkers. The sprinkling of male members may feel somewhat uncomfortable in this women's world; therefore stag groups for men only have been established for those who desire such affiliation.

The organizational structure of an Al-Anon Family Group is similar to a local A.A. unit. A chairman and a secretary are basic requirements. Larger groups may have an advisory committee and a treasurer. The more elaborate groups have a program committee, a committee on speakers, a nominating committee, and even a refreshment committee. All officers and committees function on a rotating basis with elections usually held every six months.

The responsibilities of the officers are comparable to those in A.A. The chairman plans the meetings in advance, either by himself or with the help of an advisory committee for programs. She leads the discussions at meetings or appoints someone else to do so.

The secretary acts as liaison between her group and Headquarters. All correspondence, including the monthly Forum and the Intergroup bulletin, is channeled through her for distribution and circulation within the group. In many cases the secretary maintains a current membership roster. During the meetings there is the traditional "break for the secretary" just as in A.A. sessions. She is also responsible for keeping an adequate supply of literature on hand to be displayed at meetings.

The treasurer keeps all records pertaining to the group's finances and attends to the collection of donations at meetings. She is also responsible for sending the group's contribution to Headquarters and Intergroup.

The advisory committee is equivalent to the A.A. steering

committee and consists of the current officers and several experienced members. It is concerned with group policy and local public relations.

Most groups hold meetings once a week, usually in the evening at 8:30 P.M. These sessions ordinarily open with a short period of silence or "quiet time" followed by a greeting to newcomers if any are present. Al-Anon recommends the following welcome:

> We welcome you to the Al-Anon Family Group and hope that in this fellowship you will find the help and friendship we have been privileged to enjoy. We would like you to feel that we understand as perhaps few can. We, too, were lonely and frustrated, but here we have found that there is no situation too difficult to be bettered, and no unhappiness too great to be lessened.

After the above welcome is read there may be a recitation of the Twelve Steps preceded by the following suggested Preamble:

> The Al-Anon Family Groups consist of relatives and friends of alcoholics who realize that by banding together they can better solve their common problems. Both before and after the alcoholic joins A.A. there is much that families can do to help the alcoholics and themselves.
>
> We urge you to try our program. Without spiritual help, living with an alcoholic is too much for most of us. We become nervous, irritable, unreasonable—our thinking becomes confused, and our perspective becomes distorted. A change in our attitude is of boundless help to the A.A. member and often is the force for good that finally inspires the alcoholic to join A.A. So there is no need for discouragement even though the alcoholic is still drinking.
>
> Rarely have we seen a family that was not greatly benefited when both husband and wife tried to live the A.A. program. Working in unity for a common purpose does more than strengthen both partners individually. It also draws them together.
>
> The Twelve Steps of A.A. which we try to follow are not easy. At first we may think that some of them are unneces-

sary; but if we are thoroughly honest with ourselves we will find that they all apply to us as well as the alcoholic. The benefit derived from a strict and constant observance of them can be limitless. We thus make ourselves ready to receive God's gift of serenity.

The types of meetings and the procedures employed are not specifically prescribed. Some general patterns and guidelines have evolved, based largely on A.A. custom and experience. Al-Anon suggests the following types of meetings for group practice:

Personal Story Meeting

One or more speakers tell how they came to believe that the Al-Anon program was a way of life for them.

Twelve Steps Meeting

The group takes up one or more of the Twelve Steps and the members discuss the application to themselves and their own problems.

Panel Discussion

Group members write anonymous questions which are answered by a panel of several members.

A.A. Speaker Meeting

An occasional talk by an A.A. member clarifies the need for adjustments and mutual cooperation in the home.

Family Adjustment Meeting

Husband and wife teams—one an alcoholic, the other a non-alcoholic—discuss the problems of home life.

Exchange Meeting

An individual or a team of speakers from another Al-Anon group.

Outside Speaker Meeting

Physicians, members of the clergy, court workers, social workers, psychiatrists, psychologists, and others may be asked to address a meeting.

Literature Meeting

A chapter from *Living With An Alcoholic* or an article from the *Forum* may be studied. At the discretion of the leader a suitable chapter from the Bible or any other helpful book, magazine, or newspaper article may be read. A discussion of the value of the Serenity Prayer and of the slogans may be helpful.

Open Meetings

Many groups hold an open meeting once a month, which alcoholics and other guests are invited to attend so that others may learn just what work is done by Al-Anon.

As in A.A. all meetings are concluded with the recitation of the Lord's Prayer.

Al-Anon contends, as does A.A., that affiliation with the movement should develop into a way of life which endures indefinitely. The basic philosophy is the same: alcoholism can only be arrested, never cured. Theoretically, the need for the assistance provided by the association extends far beyond the point of achievement of sobriety by the alcoholic family member, should such recovery take place. The emotional problems persist, and active membership in the group is recommended in order to avoid any "slips." Many Al-Anons still have drinking alcoholics in their homes, in which case the need for sustained and uninterrupted participation in the fellowship appears obvious. Some wives and husbands may undertake some precipitous action such as divorce from their drinking mates. However, in most cases family members cannot disengage themselves from the inevitable consequences of alcoholic behavior as it has affected them in the past, as it has an impact on their lives in the present, and as it may influence them in the future.

ALATEEN GROUPS

The Alateen movement derived from the Al-Anon program and has been established for teen-age children of alcoholics. The first Alateen group originated in Pasadena, California, in

1957 by a young man called Bob whose father was an alcoholic. Bob was having serious difficulty in his life and was completely upset by his father's drinking. His mother, a member of Al-Anon, persuaded him to try some remedial action. He began attending A.A. meetings with his parents and went to Al-Anon meetings with his mother. Although he received some help, he was not completely satisfied by these adult sessions. He conceived of a plan for organizing a group of teen-age children of members of Alcoholics Anonymous which ultimately became the first Alateen unit. Al-Anon and A.A. members helped the group in its early days and within one year it grew from five to twenty-three active participants.

The age range in Alateen is from thirteen to nineteen years, although some groups have broadened this to ages twelve to twenty. If the group is large enough it may be divided so that the younger members meet separately from the older teenagers. Any youngster interested in joining Alateen is referred to the group nearest him by Al-Anon Headquarters or Intergroup. Although Alateen is a separate program, it is to a great extent guided and watched over by Al-Anon.

Most Alateen groups are self-supporting but because many youngsters do not have sufficient funds, Al-Anon or A.A. members may make some modest contributions if needed. In some cases Alateen purchases its own literature while other expenses are met by an adult group.

Alateen officers are selected and function in the same way as in Al-Anon. Meetings are usually held in those places which house Al-Anon groups. Occasionally sessions are held in the homes of members.

Similar to Al-Anon, meetings usually open with a period of silence and conclude with the Lord's Prayer. The following preamble is also suggested for beginning the session:

The Alateen groups are made up of children of problem drinkers who find that meeting with other children of alcoholics is helpful. We realize that even though the alcoholic parent may have joined A.A., and the non-alcoholic joined Al-Anon, we, as their children, can play an important part in reuniting the family.

We urge you to try our program. We in Alateen, have learned to become individuals. We try to accept the fact that alcoholism is a disease. In studying the Twelve Steps of Alcoholics Anonymous we can accept the fact that we are powerless over alcohol, and that we can develop the ability to detach ourselves emotionally from our parents' problems, yet retain our love for them.

Our changed attitude might possibly inspire the alcoholic to seek help which may eventually lead him to A.A.; so there is no need for discouragement even though the alcoholic may still be drinking.

We try at all times to reassure our parents that we do not discuss them at our meetings. Our sole topic is the solution to our own problems.

We will always be grateful to Alateen for giving us a way of life and a wonderful, healthy program to live by and enjoy.

It is recommended that the meetings themselves be devoted to any of the following activities:

Discussion of the Twelve Steps or Traditions.

A guest speaker may be invited from Al-Anon or A.A., or a judge, clergyman, or professional person may be asked to speak.

Discussion of Al-Anon literature, appropriate magazine articles, newspaper stories, and books.

Discussion of personal problems resulting from living with an alcoholic parent (not a statement of grievances).

Business meetings.

Although some groups occasionally sponsor social activities such as parties or dances, such functions are generally discouraged as not being in keeping with the central purpose of the movement.

Alateen utilizes the Twelve Steps of A.A. just as they are

written. The Twelve Traditions of Alateen are virtually identical with the Al-Anon formulation.

The available evidence indicates that Alateen is undergoing some difficulty in establishing itself and expanding its program. Youngsters do seem to be beset with certain complications with respect to organizational affiliation to cope with the problems of their parents' drinking. Even if they do affiliate they will eventually grow up and out of the association. Alateen thus faces a more intricate problem concerning its perpetuation.

As is the case with A.A. there are no valid statistics with respect to total membership in Al-Anon and Alateen. It is apparent, however, that both organizations have grown considerably and have become useful allies in the continuing battle against the ravages of alcoholism.

Notes

Notes

NOTES FOR INTRODUCTION

1. *A.A. Exchange Bulletin*, 5 (September, 1960), pp. 1-4.

2. *Fortune*, with the collaboration of Russel W. Davenport, *U.S.A. The Permanent Revolution* (New York: Prentice-Hall, 1951), pp. 147-48.

3. Sherwood D. Fox, "Voluntary Associations and Social Structure" (unpublished Ph.D. dissertation, Harvard University, 1953, pp. 59-68).

4. David L. Sills, *The Volunteers, Means and Ends in a National Organization* (Glencoe, Illinois: The Free Press, 1957), p. 3.

5. Erving Goffman, "Characteristics of Total Institutions," in *Symposium on Preventive and Social Psychiatry* (Washington: United States Printing Office, 1957), pp. 43-84.

6. *Ibid.*, p. 44.

7. *Ibid.*, p. 45.

8. E. Wight Bakke, *Bonds of Organization* (New York: Harper and Brothers, 1950), p. 8.

9. Talcott Parsons, "Suggestions for a Sociological Approach to the Theory of Organizations" in Amitai Etzioni (ed.), *Complex Organizations* (New York: Holt, Rinehart and Winston, 1961), pp. 32-47.

10. The pathological aspects of alcoholism has been the favorite subject for scientific and non-scientific inquiry. Speaking of this, Bacon comments: "Can't stop drinkers have had their glands, livers, metabolic functioning, their anxieties, inhibitions and complexes dissected, measured, toned up and tuned down. The intuition-plus-experiment manipulators have filled alcoholics with gold and with emetics, have tapped the spine, exorcised the Freudian demons, removed allergic complexities, substituted non-alcoholic sedatives and tranquilizers for the sedating and tranquilizing alcohols, have done, in fact, almost anything one can imagine. However, when controlled experiments were instituted, it usually appeared that no very significant effects could be found." See Selden D. Bacon, "Alcoholics Do Not Drink," *The Annals of the American Academy of Political and Social Science*, 315 (January, 1958), p. 56.

The writer believes with Bacon that sociologists should direct their attention to "the customs of drinking, the relationships between these customs and other customs, the way in which drinking habits are learned, the social controls of this sort of behavior, and those institutions of society through which such control issues." See Selden D. Bacon, *Sociology and the Problems of Alcohol* (New Haven: Hillhouse Press, 1946), p. 14. In other words the sociologist should not be unduly preoccupied with the pathology of alcohol usage but rather with the social and cultural characteristics of such conduct.

11. Hugh S. Thompson, "An Experience of a Non-Alcoholic in Alcoholics Anonymous," *Quarterly Journal of Studies on Alcohol,* 13 (June, 1952), pp. 271-95.

12. Robert Freed Bales, "The Therapeutic Role of Alcoholics Anonymous as Seen by a Sociologist," *Quarterly Journal of Studies on Alcohol,* 5 (September, 1944), pp. 267-78.

13. Selden Bacon, "A Sociologist Looks at A.A.," *Minnesota Welfare,* 10 (Fall, 1957), pp. 35-44.

14. Harrison M. Trice, "Alcoholics Anonymous," *The Annals of the American Academy of Political and Social Science,* 315 (January, 1958), pp. 108-16.

15. Mary Martha Murphy, "Social Class Differences in Responsiveness to the Program of Alcoholics Anonymous" (unpublished Ph.D. dissertation, University of Chicago, June, 1952); and Wallace T. McAfee, "Alcoholics Anonymous: An Evaluative Study" (unpublished Ph.D. dissertation, University of Chicago, December, 1952).

16. Alan D. Buttin, "Psychodynamics of Alcoholism," *Quarterly Journal of Studies on Alcoholism,* 17 (June, 1956), pp. 443-60.

17. Herbert S. Shipley, Joan Jackson, Frederick F. Boyes, "Therapeutic Factors in Alcoholics Anonymous," *American Journal of Psychiatry,* 116 (July, 1959), pp. 44-50.

18. Harrison M. Trice, "Alcoholism, Group Factors in Etiology and Cure," *Human Organization,* 15 (Summer, 1957), pp. 33-40.

19. Harrison M. Trice, "A Study of the Process of Affiliation with Alcoholics Anonymous," *Quarterly Journal of Studies on Alcohol,* 18 (March, 1957), pp. 39-54; "The Affiliation Motive and Readiness to Join Alcoholics Anonymous," *Quarterly Journal of Studies on Alcohol,* 20 (June, 1959), pp. 313-20.

20. John Lofland and Robert Lejeune, "Initial Interaction of Newcomers in Alcoholics Anonymous: A Field Experiment in Class Symbols and Socialization," *Social Problems,* 8 (Fall, 1960), pp. 102-11.

21. Going out on a call from an alcoholic asking for help.

22. George C. Homans, *The Human Group* (New York: Harcourt, Brace and Company, 1950), p. 18.

23. *Ibid.,* p. 23.

NOTES FOR CHAPTER ONE

1. The principal source of the material in this chapter is derived from *Alcoholics Anonymous Comes of Age* (New York: Alcoholics Anonymous Publishing, Inc., 1957).

2. *Alcoholics Anonymous Comes of Age* (New York: Alcoholics Anonymous Publishing, Inc., 1957), p. 63.

3. *Ibid.*, p. 58.

4. *Ibid.*, p. 50.

5. Bill W., *Alcoholics Anonymous* (New York: Works Publishing, Inc., 1939).

6. *Alcoholics Anonymous Comes of Age, op. cit.*, p. 184.

7. The A.A. name for the volume.

8. *The A. A. Grapevine* (New York: Alcoholics Anonymous Publishing, Inc.).

9. *Twelve Steps and Twelve Traditions* (New York: Alcoholics Anonymous Publishing, Inc., 1953).

10. Bill W., *Alcoholics Anonymous* (2nd ed.: New York: Alcoholics Anonymous Publishing, Inc., 1955).

NOTES FOR CHAPTER TWO

1. Isolated A.A. members who are not able to participate in group activities, usually because of geographic reasons.

2. Bill W., *Alcoholics Anonymous* (New York: Works Publishing, Inc., 1939).

3. See special A.A. bibliography.

4. *The Third Legacy Manual of A.A. World Service* (New York: Alcoholics Anonymous Publishing, Inc., 1955).

5. *Twelve Steps and Twelve Traditions* (New York: Alcoholics Anonymous Publishing, Inc., 1955).

6. *Ibid.*, p. 133.

7. *Ibid.*, p. 136.

8. *Ibid.*, p. 143.

9. *Alcoholics Anonymous Comes of Age* (New York: Alcoholics Anonymous Publishing, Inc., 1957), p. 103.

10. *Twelve Steps and Twelve Traditions, op. cit.*, p. 150.

11. *Alcoholics Anonymous Comes of Age, op. cit.*, p. 105.

12. *Ibid.*, p. 106.

13. *Twelve Steps and Twelve Traditions, op. cit.*, p. 154.

14. *Ibid.*, p. 159.

15. *Alcoholics Anonymous Comes of Age, op. cit.*, p. 111.

16. *Twelve Steps and Twelve Traditions, op. cit.*, p. 164.

17. *Ibid.*, p. 170.

18. *Ibid.*, p. 176.

19. *Alcoholics Anonymous Comes of Age, op. cit.*, p. 118.

20. *Twelve Steps and Twelve Traditions, op. cit.*, p. 180.

21. Francis W. McPeek, "The Role of Religious Bodies in the Treatment of Inebriety in the United States," in *Alcohol, Science and Society* (New Haven: Quarterly Journal of Studies on Alcohol, 1945), pp. 408-12.

22. *Alcoholics Anonymous Comes of Age, op. cit.*, p. 127.

23. *Twelve Steps and Twelve Traditions, op. cit.*, p. 184.

24. *Alcoholics Anonymous Fact File* (New York: Alcoholics Anonymous Publishing, Inc., 1956).

25. *Twelve Steps and Twelve Traditions, op. cit.*, p. 188.

NOTES FOR CHAPTER THREE

1. A member who assumes the responsibility of looking after a newcomer to A.A.

2. A newcomer in A.A. who places himself under the guidance and care of a "sponsor."

3. Starts drinking again.

4. *The Third Legacy Manual of A.A. World Service* (New York: Alcoholics Anonymous Publishing, Inc., 1955).

NOTES FOR CHAPTER FOUR

1. Without a drink.

2. The low point in the alcoholic's drinking history at which time the decision is made to seek help for the problem.

3. See Appendix.

NOTES FOR CHAPTER SIX

1. John Lofland and Robert Lejeune, "Initial Interaction of Newcomers in Alcoholics Anonymous," *Social Problems*, 8 (Fall, 1960), pp. 102-11.

2. Harrison M. Trice, "Alcoholics Anonymous," *The Annals of the American Academy of Political and Social Science*, 315 (January, 1958), pp. 108-16.

3. Non-alcoholics.

4. Identifies himself as an alcoholic.

5. *Twelve Steps and Twelve Traditions* (New York: Alcoholics Anonymous Publishing, Inc., 1958), p. 109.

NOTES FOR CHAPTER SEVEN

1. Albert K. Cohen, "The Study of Social Disorganization and Deviant Behavior," in *Sociology Today*, Robert Merton, *et al.*, eds. (New York: Basic Books, 1959), p. 462.

2. Frederick M. Thrasher, *The Gang* (Chicago: University of Chicago Press, 1936) 2nd ed., p. 278.

3. *Ibid.*, p. 297.

4. William F. Whyte, *Street Corner Society* (Chicago: University of Chicago Press, 1943), p. 256.

5. Robert Dubin, "Deviant Behavior and Social Structure: Continuities in Social Theory," *American Sociological Review*, 24 (April, 1959), p. 147.

6. Albert K. Cohen, *Delinquent Boys* (Glencoe, Illinois: The Free Press, 1955).

7. Howard S. Becker, "Marihuana Use and Social Control," *Social Problems*, 3 (July, 1955), p. 35.

8. *Ibid.*, p. 36.

9. Robert Merton, *Social Theory and Social Structure* (Glencoe, Illinois: The Free Press, 1957), 2nd. ed., p. 121.

10. *Ibid.*, p. 134.

11. Richard A. Cloward, "Illegitimate Means, Anomie, and Deviant Behavior," *American Sociological Review*, 24 (April, 1959), p. 167.

12. Dubin, *op. cit.*, p. 162.

13. *Ibid.*, p. 156.

14. Talcott Parsons, *The Social System* (Glencoe, Illinois: The Free Press, 1951), p. 292.

15. *Ibid.*, p. 293.

16. See Max Weber, *The Theory of Social and Economic Organization* (translated by A. M. Henderson and Talcott Parsons; New York: Oxford University Press, 1947).

17. Alvin W. Gouldner, "Organizational Analysis" in *Sociology Today*, Robert Merton, *et al.*, eds. (New York: Basic Books, 1959), p. 403.

18. David L. Sills, *The Volunteers: Means and Ends in a National Organization* (Glencoe, Illinois: The Free Press, 1957), p. 65.

19. Robert A. Dentler and Kai T. Erickson, "The Functions of Deviance in Group," *Social Problems*, 7 (Fall, 1959), p. 106.

20. *Ibid.*, p. 107.

21. Richard T. LaPiere, *A Theory of Social Control* (New York: McGraw-Hill Book Co., 1954), p. 118.

22. The Twelve Steps and Twelve Traditions may be found listed in almost all A.A. literature.

23. An alcoholic who has not suffered severely because of his drinking. One who has usually not been jailed or hospitalized.

24. An alcoholic who has suffered severely and may have spent time living in "skid row." The "bottom" is the point from which recovery begins.

25. Dentler and Erickson, *op. cit.*, p. 107.

26. Marshall Clinard, *Sociology of Deviant Behavior* (New York: Rinehart and Company, 1957), p. 11.

NOTES FOR CHAPTER EIGHT

1. Raymond J. Corsini, *Methods of Group Psychotherapy* (New York: McGraw-Hill Book Co., 1957), p. 5.

2. Selden Bacon, "A Sociologist Looks at A.A.," *Minnesota Welfare*, 10 (Fall, 1957), pp. 35-44.

3. Howard J. Clinebell, Jr., *Understanding and Counseling the Alcoholic Through Religion and Psychology* (New York: Abingdon Press, 1956), p. 164.

4. Jerome D. Frank, "Group Methods in Psychotherapy" in Arnold Rose (ed.), *Mental Health and Mental Disorder* (New York: W. W. Norton, Co., 1955), pp. 524-35.

5. *Ibid.*, p. 530.

6. *Ibid.*, p. 531.

7. *Ibid.*

8. *Ibid.*

9. *Ibid.*, p. 532

NOTES FOR CHAPTER NINE

1. Bernard Barber, "Participation and Mass Apathy in Associations," in Alvin W. Gouldner (ed.), *Studies in Leadership* (New York: Harper and Brothers, 1950), p. 488.

2. David L. Sills, *The Volunteers: Means and Ends in National Organization* (Glencoe, Illinois: The Free Press, 1957), p. 26.

3. See Nathan E. Cohen (ed.), *The Citizen Volunteer: His Responsibility, Role and Opportunity in Modern Society* (New York: Harper and Brothers, 1960).

4. Barber, *op. cit.,* p. 489.

5. *Ibid.*

6. *Alcoholics Anonymous Comes of Age* (New York: Alcoholics Anonymous Publishing, Inc., 1957), pp. 130-31.

7. *Ibid.,* p. 227.

8. Arnold M. Rose, *Sociology* (New York: Alfred A. Knopf, 1956), p. 317.

9. F. Stuart Chapin, "The Growth of Bureaucracy: An Hypothesis," *American Sociological Review,* 16 (December, 1951), p. 835.

10. F. Stuart Chapin and John E. Tsouderos, "The Formalization Process in Voluntary Associations," *Social Forces,* 34 (May, 1956), p. 343.

11. John E. Tsouderos, "Organizational Change in Terms of a Series of Selected Variables," *American Sociological Review,* 20 (April, 1955), pp. 206-10.

12. Rose, *op. cit.,* p. 305.

13. *Ibid.,* p. 306.

14. Sills, *op. cit.,* p. 35.

15. Barber, *op. cit.,* p. 486.

16. Sills, *op. cit.,* p. 36.

17. Kenneth E. Boulding, *The Organizational Revolution* (New York: Harper and Brothers, 1953), p. 11; David B. Truman, *The Governmental Process* (New York: Alfred A. Knopf, 1951), pp. 157-67.

NOTES FOR CHAPTER TEN

1. Erving Goffman, "Characteristics of Total Institutions" in *Symposium on Preventive and Social Psychiatry* (Washington: United States Printing Office, 1957).

2. *Ibid.,* p. 65.

NOTES FOR CHAPTER ELEVEN

1. Hadley Cantril, *The Psychology of Social Movements* (New York: John Wiley and Sons, 1951), p. 145.

2. *Ibid.,* p. 147.

3. *Ibid.,* p. 160.

4. Purnell Handy Benson, *Religion in Contemporary Culture* (New York: Harper and Brothers, 1960), p. 323.

5. *Twelve Steps and Twelve Traditions* (New York: Alcoholics Anonymous Publishing, Inc., 1953), p. 28.

6. Harry M. Tiebout, "Therapeutic Mechanisms of Alcoholics

Anonymous," *American Journal of Psychiatry* (January, 1944), pp. 469-70.

7. G. Aiken Taylor, *A Sober Faith: Religion and Alcoholics Anonymous* (New York: The Macmillan Co., 1953), p. 35.

8. *Ibid.*, p. 106.

9. Benson, *op. cit.*, p. 613.

10. Elizabeth K. Nottingham, *Religion and Society* (New York: Random House, 1954), p. 4.

11. Benson, *op. cit.*, p. 605.

12. *Ibid.*, p. 607.

13. Nottingham, *op. cit.*, p. 8.

14. From the special program for the Three Day Farewell at the Old Site, February, 1960.

15. Bill W., *Alcoholics Anonymous* (New York: Works Publishing, Inc., 1939).

16. The author is indebted to John Lofland for the stimulating ideas developed in his unpublished manuscript "On Creating and Maintaining Involvement in Alcoholics Anonymous: Some Observations on Manhattan A.A.," June, 1961.

17. Nottingham, *op. cit.*, pp. 60-61.

NOTES FOR APPENDIX

1. The author is indebted to several members of the Al-Anon Family Group Headquarters for information provided during a detailed interview. In addition, much of the material for this chapter is derived from various Al-Anon publications, principally *Living With An Alcoholic* (New York, Al-Anon Family Group Headquarters, Inc., 1962), and the *Manual for Al-Anon Family Groups* (New York: Al-Anon Family Group Headquarters, Inc., 1962).

2. See special Al-Anon bibliography.

Index

Index